COWBOY
REPUBLIC

COWBOY REPUBLIC

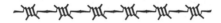

SIX WAYS THE BUSH GANG
HAS DEFIED THE LAW

MARJORIE COHN

Foreword by Richard Falk

PoliPointPress

Cowboy Republic: Six Ways the Bush Gang Has Defied the Law

Copyright © 2007 by Marjorie Cohn

This edition published in the United States of America by
PoliPointPress, P.O. Box 3008, Sausalito, CA 94966-3008
www.p3books.com

Production management: BookMatters
Cover design: Jeff Kenyon
Print date: June 2007
Distributed by Ingram Publisher Services Inc.

Library of Congress Cataloging in Publication Data
    Cohn, Marjorie, 1948–
    Cowboy republic : six ways the Bush gang has defied the law /
Marjorie Cohn ; foreword by Richard Falk.
        p.   cm.
     Includes bibliographical references and index.
        ISBN 978-0-9778253-3-2 (alk. paper)
        1. Bush, George W. (George Walker), 1946–
    2.   Executive power—United States.   3.   Iraq War, 2003–
    4.   Torture—United States.   5.   Civil rights—United States.
    I. Title.
    JK511.C635   2007
    973.931—dc22   2007009252

Printed in the United States of America

Published by:
PoliPointPress, LLC
P.O. Box 3008
Sausalito, CA 94966-3008
(415) 339-4100
www.p3books.com

To my parents
Leonard and Florence Cohn
and my children
Victor and Nicolas Cohn-López

Contents

Foreword

The dismal experience of the Iraq War should contain many lessons for Americans, but the most important may be that adhering to international law serves the national (as well human) interest in times of war. Such a lesson is still not part of our national conversation. Even the most respected newspapers rarely discuss the legality of American foreign policy. The *New York Times*, for instance, generally regarded as the gold standard of the media world, covered the run-up to the war lavishly but gave no editorial space to those who opposed the invasion on the grounds that it violated international law and the UN Charter. It printed column after column on justifications for the war and matters of feasibility and tactics, but it rejected pieces by distinguished jurists questioning its legality.

It is discouraging to note that the same pattern applied to the Vietnam War. Toward the end, some observers noted that if international law had guided American policy, the United States would have avoided a humiliating defeat and the Vietnamese people a tragic ordeal. Yet the dominant lesson from that war was later called, disparagingly, "the Vietnam syndrome." Defeat recoded as "syndrome" expressed a national reluctance to commit to warfare abroad. Subsequent American presidents, whether

Republican or Democratic, regarded the Vietnam syndrome as an unwelcome constraint on the use of American power during the latter stages of the Cold War. It is noteworthy that the first words of then-President George H. W. Bush after the defeat of Iraq in 1991 were, "We finally kicked the Vietnam syndrome," meaning the United States could again go to war without violating its comfort zone. This may have been good news at the Pentagon and American Enterprise Institute, but it was terrible news for the peoples of the Third World, especially those in the Middle East.

What the Vietnam War might have taught, and what the Iraq War should certainly teach, is that defying international law can be a costly choice with disastrous political and economic consequences, especially when the violation produces massive bloodshed and widespread devastation. Another lesson, not widely heeded, is that international law is not the work of utopians or dreamy idealists; rather, it represents the efforts of experienced diplomats to protect the interests of all states. For many years, the United States was at the forefront of these practical efforts to impose legal limits on recourse to war, having been long convinced that the endless cycle of warfare in Europe was extremely wasteful, destructive, and demoralizing. Sadly, Europe is now seen as valuing international law to a much higher degree than is the United States.

In *Of Paradise and Power*, the neoconservative heavyweight Robert Kagan argues that it is the luxury of the weak to be law-minded and the responsibility of the strong to be power-oriented. Such false guidance can produce only failure after failure when the weapons of the weak can neutralize, and often defeat, the military power of the strong. Of course, his argument also obscures the fact that respect for international law would have prevented two American foreign policy disasters. Kagan and others cannot see that the law helpfully shapes the use of power on the global stage and that adherence to it does not disadvantage the state. This lesson is not meant for America only. It applies also to the Soviet invasion of Afghanistan in 1979, to Iraq's invasion of Iran in 1980 and conquest of Kuwait in 1990, and to Israel's assault on Lebanon in 2006. We have reached a point in the relations between power, politics, and warfare where the mediation of international law is essential for rational behavior.

I do not wish to suggest that aggressive war is more acceptable when it achieves its strategic results. Putting the point provocatively, the one thing worse than chaos and defeat in Iraq would have been a decisive and quick American victory. Why? Such an outcome would have encouraged the further pursuit of imperial goals by recourse to war and spread the war zone to other Middle East targets in the neoconservative gun sights.

Behind pragmatic calculations about victory and defeat are moral determinations of right and wrong. International law has moved over time to take account of these determinations, especially in the aftermath of what were generally perceived to be disastrous wars. The League of Nations came after World War I, the United Nations and Nuremberg came after World War II, The Geneva Conventions and Protocols came after World War II and the Vietnam War. International law encodes prevailing sentiments about right and wrong and gradually provides the means for their implementation.

A momentous step was taken after the defeat of Hitler's Germany. The Nuremberg trials convicted surviving Germans responsible for aggressive war and other abuses. These trials were widely criticized as "victors' justice," and so they were. Nothing was done, for instance, to impose criminal responsibility for the massive violations of the laws of war associated with the bombing of German and Japanese cities by the Allied Powers, which deliberately targeted civilian populations in crowded urban areas. The American prosecutor at Nuremberg, Robert Jackson (on leave from his normal duties as U.S. Supreme Court Justice), eloquently stated that the punishment inflicted on the German defendants would not be seen as justice unless those who sit in judgment bind their own future conduct by the same standards: "We must never forget that the record on which we judge these defendants today is the record on which history will judge us tomorrow. To pass these defendants a poisoned chalice is to put it to our own lips as well." This Nuremberg promise has been broken repeatedly, especially by the United States.

Many of these legal issues emerged forcefully after the 9/11 attacks, which allowed neoconservatives to push their extremist agenda at home and abroad. Under the cover of "counterterrorism" or "the war on terror," previously unimaginable abuses of power have taken place under the auspices of the U.S. government—often with the blessings of government lawyers. Indeed, those lawyers justified a dazzling array of shameless acts, including torture and "rendering" detainees to governments known for severely abusive interrogations. Post-9/11 tribal patriotism invited legal scoundrels to come out of the closet! And sadly, they came out in droves. This dark honor roll includes Alberto Gonzales, John Yoo, Jack Goldsmith, Jay Bybee, and William J. Haynes.

Against this backdrop, Marjorie Cohn's commentaries on the Iraq experience are a national treasure, embodying calm, incisive, accurate, and altogether devastating accounts of the numerous ways the Bush presidency has undermined constitutional government and our sense of human decency. Professor Cohn also helps us to understand why the Iraq War is a flagrant example of an aggressive war, which was considered "the supreme international crime" at Nuremburg. Such a book should be required reading for members of the U.S. Congress, for those who shape the news, and indeed for anyone who wants to understand why being a good American citizen at this time has become almost synonymous with adopting a posture of resistance.

Professor Cohn approvingly writes about Lt. Ehren Watada, who faces imprisonment because he refuses to obey an order to be deployed in Iraq. She shows the incredible catch-22 circumstance that confronts this young soldier, and indeed the entire American military, whether they realize it or not. Either Lt. Watada obeys the provision of the U.S. Army Field Manual 27-10 obliging him to disobey an unlawful order—a choice that will likely send him to prison for refusing to follow a command—or he participates in an illegal war of aggression that could potentially make him liable for criminal prosecution. When the law requires a person to swallow his conscience, we know the political atmosphere has been severely tainted. But when the legal system requires a person to choose between two unlawful courses of action, perhaps with lethal consequences, the whole system is awry and becomes a recipe for collective schizophrenia. The dilemma is accentuated by the military court's refusal to allow Lt. Watada even to introduce evidence on the illegality of the war and thereby explain his unwillingness to obey the command to deploy.

We can only be thankful that we have brave citizens of moral and legal clarity such as Ehren Watada and Marjorie Cohn, who remind us by their vivid words and deeds that international law is worth taking seriously—not only for self-serving reasons, but also for the welfare of the country and the world. Fortunately, there have been many others with professional legal backgrounds who have defended detainees abused at the Guantánamo Bay prison and elsewhere and who believe that international law and human rights are precious pillars of genuine constitutional democracy. President Bush likes to call the war on terror the great ideological struggle of our time; but truly, if there is such a struggle, it is to establish some form of humane global governance that incorporates at its core the rule of law— and then enforces it vigorously against the strong as well as the weak. If this struggle is lost, the Iraq War in all its ugliness and criminality will doom our future. Marjorie Cohn's fine book should inspire us to wage this struggle for a better future with all the energy at our disposal.

Richard Falk
Santa Barbara, California
January 25, 2007

-)(((—)((—)((-

INTRODUCTION

The American cowboy is by now a richly symbolic, even mythical, figure. The hero of countless movies and dime novels, he has become an international icon of rugged independence, freedom, and self-sufficiency. But at least one dictionary definition of *cowboy* is less flattering. According to *Webster's*, a cowboy is also one "who undertakes a dangerous or sensitive task needlessly." In a rodeo, that kind of danger is part of the appeal. But in national politics, this cowboy ethic clashes with an even more basic American tradition: a distaste for tyrants. Long before six-shooters and ten-gallon hats became the rage, the Founding Fathers were making sure that our system of checks and balances would prevent presidents (and other public officials) from going off half-cocked.

Perhaps the most important protection against cowboy bravado is the U.S. Constitution, which carefully divides political and legal powers among the three branches of government. Even if a cowboy manages to become president, he still needs congressional approval for his shootouts. And if he turns out to be an overzealous vigilante instead of a reliable enforcer of the nation's laws, the courts and Congress can rein him in. As a law professor and president of the National Lawyers Guild, I'm a true believer

1

in the Constitution. It's the foundation of our political and legal system, and when I see it violated, I consider it my duty to speak out. In my view, this is what Thomas Jefferson had in mind when he called dissent "the highest form of patriotism."

Historians and legal scholars know that this kind of dissent is often necessary. In 1798, the Federalist-led Congress, capitalizing on the fear of war, passed the four Alien and Sedition Acts to stifle dissent against the Federalist Party's agenda. The Sedition Act, rushed through Congress, provided criminal penalties for any person who wrote, printed, published, or spoke anything "false, scandalous and malicious" with the intent to hold the government in "contempt or disrepute." The Federalists argued it was necessary to suppress criticism of the government in time of war. Employed exclusively against Republicans, the Act was used to target congressmen and newspaper editors who criticized President John Adams. This wasn't our finest moment, but our First Amendment protections eventually prevailed.

During the Second World War, the U.S. government decided to round up more than 100,000 people of Japanese descent living on the West Coast and place them in concentration camps. Virtually no public officials or mainstream media figures objected; even Earl Warren, who would become the foremost progressive jurist of the twentieth century, supported the measure at the time. Most of the evacuees were U.S. citizens, but the Supreme Court ruled in 1944 that their internment was constitutional. Although that court decision still stands, Congress finally apologized in 1988 for this "grave injustice" that was "motivated largely by racial prejudice, wartime hysteria, and a failure of political leadership." That episode is now another painful reminder that wartime fears frequently lead to decisions that betray our core principles.

In the 1950s, our government succumbed to Cold War fears

hyped by Senator Joseph McCarthy and others. In pursuit of real and imagined communists, the government took actions that led to thousands of lost jobs and ruined lives. Fear pervaded every facet of life, leading neighbors to inform on one another. CBS newscaster Edward R. Murrow was one of the few journalists who had the courage to stand up to the fear-mongering and bring the truth to the American people. Describing the omnipresent fear that the government was fostering, Murrow told his colleagues, "The terror's in the room." In the end, that terror was reduced only when courageous citizens (and, behind the scenes, the Eisenhower administration) finally resisted McCarthy's witch hunt.

As these and other examples demonstrate, Americans haven't always lived up to the principles enshrined in the Constitution. But these episodes also show that our best hope lies in demanding that our government adhere to these principles. That need is especially acute when it concerns the executive branch, whose job it is to enforce the law. If members of the executive branch fail to do that—or, worse, if they're breaking the law themselves—our political system can be thrown into crisis, to the detriment of the people.

A second set of protections against irresponsible government was erected after the Second World War. Having endured European fascism, genocide, and the bloodiest conflict in history, postwar governments tried leaders for war crimes and thereby set a series of international legal precedents. These governments, led by the United States, also ratified the Charter of the United Nations to prevent wanton state violence in future conflicts. Like the U.S. Constitution, the UN Charter has been violated many times since then. But by promoting and ratifying them, the U.S. government explicitly agreed to abide by—and enforce—their provisions.

Many Americans don't understand that much of international law is actually U.S. law. Indeed, the Supremacy Clause of the Constitution says that treaties shall be the supreme law of the land. When the United States became a party to the UN Charter, it agreed to respect the principle of sovereign equality of all nations. That means settling disputes so that international peace, security, and justice are not endangered. The Charter requires UN members to refrain from the threat or use of force against the territorial integrity or political independence of any other country. One country can invade another only in self-defense or with the Security Council's blessing. Unilateral, preemptive wars are wars of aggression. The UN Charter calls those wars a *crime against peace;* at Nuremberg, they called them the Supreme International Crime.

The United States is also party to the Convention Against Torture and Other Cruel, Inhuman or Degrading Treatment or Punishment. That treaty outlaws torture in all circumstances, even in time of war. The International Covenant on Civil and Political Rights and the Geneva Conventions, also ratified by the United States, prohibit torture and degrading treatment as well. Two of our federal laws, the War Crimes Act and the Torture Statute, are based on our treaty obligations. They carry life in prison, and even the death penalty, for those who violate them. Under the doctrine of *command responsibility,* commanders—all the way up the chain of command to the commander in chief—can be held liable for torture and war crimes. If they knew or should have known their subordinates would commit the offenses, and the commanders did nothing to stop or prevent them, the commanders are just as culpable as those who carried out the prohibited acts.

When followed, the U.S. Constitution, UN Charter, and international treaties provide a great deal of protection against cowboy indiscretions. But even they didn't prevent a series of executive branch violations in the 1960s and 1970s, when the Vietnam War, Watergate, and intelligence and law enforcement abuses demonstrated that executive branch power had exceeded the limits set by the Founding Fathers. After several years of Senate hearings, Congress passed measures to strengthen its oversight of the FBI, CIA, and the White House. One of these measures was the Foreign Intelligence Surveillance Act (FISA), which requires the executive branch to seek court warrants for domestic wiretapping.

Many Bush administration officials, including Vice President Dick Cheney, have suggested that the measures taken during the 1970s were themselves unconstitutional constraints on executive power. But like the U.S. Constitution, the UN Charter, and the Geneva Conventions, these laws were not passed in a historical vacuum; rather, they were direct responses to actual abuses, and they were designed to prevent future abuses. Unless and until they're modified, they remain the law of the land.

I became politically active when many of these abuses were occurring. For example, I was one of thousands of students who opposed an illegal war in Vietnam. When I arrived at college, awash in the wisdom and experience of a high school cheerleader and homecoming princess, I couldn't have imagined how that war would change me. I was raised to believe my government was beyond reproach. But a grainy black-and-white film I saw as a Stanford freshman turned the tide for me. In the film, a young Vietnamese girl was running down the road, naked and screaming, because an American warplane had just dropped napalm on her. I felt a wrenching in my gut. I knew it was my responsibility to help stop the war. I joined the antiwar movement and participated in a sit-in at Stanford's Applied Electronics Laboratory, which was doing research on chemical and biological warfare and counterinsurgency in Southeast Asia. For me, dissent against that war was the most patriotic thing I could do.

After many years of legal study and activism, I'm even more committed to our Constitution and civil liberties. But you don't have to be a law professor to see that our leaders are once again undertaking dangerous and sensitive tasks needlessly. In doing so, they're betraying our nation's core principles, breaking the law they swore to enforce, violating the Constitution they pledged to protect, and undermining treaties our government drafted and ratified.

As this book goes to press, the courts and Congress seem to be curbing some of the more obvious infractions committed by the Bush gang. Congress passed a bill that would bring the troops home from Iraq in 2008, but President George W. Bush vetoed it. The Supreme Court handed down a trio of decisions that will go down in history as some of the most significant statements on the limits of executive power. In *Hamdi v. Rumsfeld*, the Court declared that "war is not a blank check" for the President. *Rasul v. Bush* held that U.S. federal courts have jurisdiction to consider habeas corpus petitions filed by the Guantánamo detainees, and *Hamdan v. Rumsfeld* affirmed that there are no gaps in the Geneva Conventions; prisoners must always be treated humanely. But the Court postponed deciding whether habeas corpus survived the new Military Commissions Act.

Yet there are also signs that the worst abuses will continue. The illegal occupation of Iraq continues, as does the illegal detention of prisoners in Guantánamo, as does the illegal rendition of detainees to third countries, where they will be tortured. And Bush is rattling his sabers again, this time in Iran's direction. I find little reason to believe the Bush gang has changed its ways. For example, the administration said it would now seek court approval for wiretapping of domestic communications but then backtracked. Likewise, President George W. Bush recently signed a bill prohibiting the government from opening mail without a court warrant; at the same time, he issued a signing statement authorizing the "opening of an item of a class of mail otherwise sealed against inspection, in a manner consistent . . . with the need to conduct searches in exigent circumstances." This statement defies the letter and spirit of the bill that he was signing into law at that very moment.

A democracy remains vibrant only when citizens know what their leaders are doing in their name. This knowledge can be elusive, largely because the Bush administration is ever more secretive. Even so, we know a great deal about this administration and its activities, and this knowledge creates a duty—not just for Congress and the courts but also for regular citizens. This duty is not new, novel, or extraordinary; indeed, it goes back to this nation's birth. When Benjamin Franklin was leaving the Constitutional Convention, a group of citizens asked what kind of government the delegates had created. "A Republic, if you can keep it," Franklin replied. This book is dedicated to that effort.

ONE

-)))(((-)))(((-)))((-

A WAR OF AGGRESSION

According to sources inside the administration, George W. Bush was planning to invade Iraq and remove its government well before the terrorist attacks of September 11, 2001.[1] Such an invasion violates the Charter of the United Nations (UN), which the United States signed in 1945 after the bloodiest conflict in history. The charter permits countries to use military force against another country only in self-defense or with Security Council permission. But the evidence indicates that the U.S.-led invasion satisfied neither condition and is therefore a war of aggression, which constitutes a *crime against peace*— exactly the kind of war the UN Charter was meant to prevent.

The Bush gang doesn't think much of the UN, unless its resolutions happen to support American policy, but that hasn't always been the official U.S. line. Calling the UN Charter "a victory against war itself," President Harry Truman noted that the victors in the Second World War had "no right to dominate the world."[2] President Bush doesn't seem to agree. Although he marketed the war in Iraq as necessary to protect us from Saddam Hussein's weapons of mass destruction (WMDs), Bush's decisions had less to do with self-defense than with dominating the oil-rich Middle East.

Some evidence for this conclusion can be found in a September 2000 report prepared by the neoconservative Project for a New American Century (PNAC). The report, commissioned by Dick Cheney, outlines a plan "to maintain American military preeminence that is consistent with the requirements of a strategy of American global leadership."[3] It notes that although "the unresolved conflict with Iraq provides the immediate justification, the need for a substantial American force presence in the Gulf transcends the issue of the regime of Saddam Hussein." Another document produced for Vice President Cheney's secret Energy Task Force included a map of Iraqi oil fields, pipelines, refineries, and terminals as well as charts detailing Iraqi oil and gas projects and "Foreign Suitors for Iraqi Oilfield Contracts."[4] That document was dated March 2001, six months before 9/11 and two years before Bush invaded Iraq.

The PNAC report admitted that the process of transforming our military so the United States would remain the world's undisputed leader was "likely to be a long one, absent some catastrophic and catalyzing event—like a new Pearl Harbor."[5] On September 11, 2001, that catastrophic event occurred when 19 men, most from Saudi Arabia, flew hijacked airplanes into the World Trade Center and the Pentagon, killing nearly 3,000 people. The administration had its new Pearl Harbor.

The Bush gang swung into action. First, they attacked Afghanistan and removed the Taliban from power.[6] But the primary target all along was Iraq. To sell the war to the American people, the administration made two claims and repeated them like a mantra. First, Iraq had WMDs. Second, it had ties with al-Qaeda and was thus complicit in the 9/11 attacks. Although the administration argued that both reasons justified the use of force against Iraq, it was advised repeatedly that neither claim was valid.

NO WEAPONS OF MASS DESTRUCTION

In 2002, former United Nations weapons inspector Scott Ritter summarized his views on Iraq's weapons program as follows:

> I believe the primary problem at this point is one of accounting. Iraq has destroyed 90–95% of its weapons of mass destruction. . . . We have to remember that this missing 5–10% doesn't necessarily constitute a threat. It doesn't even constitute a weapons program. . . . Likewise, just because we can't account for it doesn't mean Iraq retains it. There's no evidence Iraq retains this material.[7]

Ritter's conclusions weren't lost on the international community. On September 10, 2002, former South African President Nelson Mandela pointed out that Ritter found "no evidence whatsoever of [development of weapons of] mass destruction" and that neither Bush nor British Prime Minister Tony Blair had "provided any evidence that such weapons exist."[8]

Six days later, Dr. Naji Sabri, Minister of Foreign Affairs of Iraq, informed UN Secretary General Kofi Annan that Iraq would allow the return of UN weapons inspectors to Iraq without conditions. Sabri further expressed Iraq's desire to complete the implementation of relevant Security Council resolutions and to remove any doubts about Iraq still possessing WMDs.[9] But as Iraq became more cooperative, Bush grew more agitated.[10] He wanted to go to war. In the end, no WMDs were found by the UN weapons inspectors before Bush invaded Iraq or by the U.S. inspection team after the invasion.[11]

How could the American claims about WMDs have been so wrong? Former U.S. Central Intelligence Agency (CIA) officials acknowledged manipulation of intelligence. Vincent Cannistraro, the CIA's former head of counterintelligence, alleged that before the war began, "Basically, cooked information is working its way into high-level pronouncements and there's a lot of unhappiness about it in intelligence, especially at the CIA."[12] Michael Scheuer, a CIA analyst, echoed this sentiment in 2005, stating, "There was just a resignation within the agency that we were going to war against Iraq and it didn't make any difference what the analysis was or what kind of objections or countervailing forces there were to an invasion. We were going to war."[13]

Similar accusations were made by Greg Thielmann, Director of Strategic Proliferation and Military Affairs Office at the State Department's Intelligence Bureau. Thielmann, who was responsible for analyzing the Iraq weapons threat, accused the White House of "systematic, across-the-board exaggeration" of intelligence to make the case that Saddam Hussein posed an imminent threat to the United States.[14] "The American public was seriously misled," Thielmann charged. "The Administration twisted, distorted, and simplified intelligence in a way that led Americans to seriously misunderstand the nature of the Iraq threat. I'm not sure I can think of a worse act against the people in a democracy than a president distorting critical classified information."[15]

An August 2006 report prepared at the direction of Rep. John Conyers, Jr., found that "members of the Bush Administration misstated, overstated, and manipulated intelligence with regards to linkages between Iraq and Al Qaeda; the acquisition of nuclear weapons by Iraq; the acquisition of aluminum tubes to be used as uranium centrifuges; and the acquisition of uranium from Niger."[16] The report also noted that "[b]eyond making false and misleading statements about Iraq's attempt to acquire nuclear weapons, the record shows the Bush Administration must have known these statements conflicted with known international and domestic intelligence at the time."[17] Finding that the administration had also misstated or overstated intelligence information regarding chemical and biological weapons, the report concluded that "these misstatements were in contradiction of known countervailing intelligence information, and were the result of political pressure and manipulation."[18] In short, the Bush gang misrepresented the WMD threat to justify its planned invasion of Iraq.

NO CONNECTION BETWEEN IRAQ AND AL-QAEDA

On September 21, 2001, Bush was told in the President's Daily Brief that the intelligence community had no evidence connecting Saddam Hussein's regime to the 9/11 attacks. Furthermore, there was scant credible evidence that Iraq had any significant collaborative ties with al-Qaeda.[19] This was no surprise. Al-Qaeda is a consortium of intensely religious Islamic fundamentalists, whereas Hussein ran a secular government that repressed religious activity in Iraq.

Undeterred, Bush and his people continued to tout the connection. Although the Defense Intelligence Agency (DIA) determined in February 2002 that "Iraq is unlikely to have provided bin Laden any useful [chemical or biological weapons] knowledge or assistance," Bush proclaimed one year later, "Iraq has also provided al-Qaeda with chemical and biological weapons training."[20] Iraq's foreign minister informed the CIA in September 2002 that Iraq never had any connection with Osama bin Laden, yet Bush declared days later, "Al-Qaeda hides. Saddam doesn't, but the danger is, is that they work in concert. The danger is, is that al-Qaeda becomes an extension of Saddam's madness and his hatred and his capacity to extend weapons of mass destruction around the world. . . . [Y]ou can't distinguish between al-Qaeda and Saddam when you talk about the war on terror."[21] And although the CIA concluded in a classified January 2003 report that Hussein "viewed Islamic extremists operating inside Iraq as a threat," Cheney claimed the next day that the Iraqi government "aids and protects terrorists, including members of al-Qaeda."[22]

To support their claims that Iraq was training al-Qaeda members, Bush, Cheney, and Colin Powell repeatedly cited information provided by Ibn al-Shaykh al-Libi, an al-Qaeda prisoner captured shortly after 9/11.[23] An ex-FBI official told *Newsweek* that the CIA "duct-taped [al-Libi's] mouth, cinched him up and sent him to Cairo" for some "more-fearsome Egyptian interrogations"[24] in violation of U.S. law prohibiting extraordinary rendition.[25] Al-Libi's account proved worthless. The February 2002 DIA memo reveals that al-Libi provided his American interrogators with false material suggesting Iraq had trained al-Qaeda to use WMDs. Even though U.S. intelligence thought the information was untrue as early as 2002 because it was obtained by torture, al-Libi's information provided the centerpiece of Colin Powell's now thoroughly discredited February 2003 claim before the United Nations that Iraq had developed WMD programs.[26]

THE MARCH TO WAR

Unable to find any WMDs or connection between Iraq and the 9/11 attacks, Bush never wavered in his march toward war. "From the very beginning," former Treasury Secretary Paul O'Neill said on *60 Minutes*, "there was a conviction that Saddam Hussein was a bad person and that he needed to go. It was all about finding a way to do it. That was the tone of it. The president saying, 'Go find me a way to do this.'"[27]

On September 15, 2001, in a meeting at Camp David, Defense Secretary Donald Rumsfeld suggested an attack on Iraq because he was deeply worried about the availability of "good targets in Afghanistan." Former Deputy Defense Secretary Paul Wolfowitz argued that war against Iraq might be "easier than against Afghanistan."[28] The "9/11 Commission Report" noted that as early as September 20, 2001, Undersecretary of Defense for Policy Douglas Feith suggested attacking Iraq in response to the 9/11 attacks.[29]

In late November 2001, Bush instructed Rumsfeld to develop an Iraq war plan. "What have you got in terms of plans for Iraq?" Bush asked. "What is the status of the war plan? I want you to get on it. I want you to keep it secret."[30] "There was a great deal of pressure to find a reason to go to war with Iraq," a CIA official working on WMDs said in late 2001. "And the pressure was not just subtle; it was blatant. . . . [The official's boss] called a meeting and gave them their marching orders. And he said, 'You know what? If Bush wants to go to war, it's your job to give him a reason to do so.'"[31]

Bush declared in his January 2002 State of the Union Address that countries like Iraq, Iran, and North Korea "constitute an axis of evil. . . . These regimes pose a grave and growing danger. . . . I will not wait on events, while dangers gather."[32] As early as February 2002, the Bush administration took concrete steps to deploy military troops and assets into Iraq without advising Congress or seeking its approval.[33] By late March, Dick Cheney told his fellow Republicans that a decision had been made to invade Iraq.[34] The same month, Bush poked his head into Condoleezza Rice's office and said, "Fuck Saddam. We're taking him out."[35]

In July 2002, a highly classified document titled "CentCom Courses of Action" was leaked to the *New York Times*. Prepared two months earlier, it contained what the Pentagon labeled a "war plan" for invading Iraq. The document, which indicated an advanced stage of planning, called for tens of thousands of marines and soldiers to attack Iraq from the air, land, and sea to topple Saddam Hussein.[36]

Bush's secret air war on Iraq began in May 2002 and intensified in August 2002.[37] The *Sunday Times* of London reported, "By the end of August [2002] the raids had become a full air offensive."[38] Former CIA analyst Ray McGovern later testified, "The step-up in bombing was incredible. In March–April of 2002, there were hardly any bombs dropped at all. By the time September came along, several hundred tons of bombs had been dropped. The war had really started."[39] Later, Lieutenant General Michael Moseley confirmed the secret war.[40]

In August 2002, Cheney cautioned that Saddam Hussein could try to dominate "the entire Middle East and subject the United States to nuclear blackmail." He added, "There is no doubt that Saddam Hussein now has weapons of mass destruction."[41] The same month, the Bush administration quietly established the White House Iraq Group (WHIG) to lead a propaganda campaign to bolster public support for war with Iraq.[42]

A week before WHIG began its work in earnest, the "Downing Street Memo" was written. It contained the secret minutes of a July 2002 meeting with Tony Blair and Sir Richard Dearlove, chief of British intelligence. Dearlove reported that Bush had already decided to go to war and was making sure "the intelligence and facts" about Iraq and WMDs "were being fixed around the policy" of war on Iraq.[43]

Shortly after WHIG convened, White House officials told the *New York Times* there was a meticulously planned strategy to sell a war against Iraq to the American people. But the White House decided to wait until after Labor Day to kick off the plan. The reason, as explained by White House chief of staff Andrew Card, seemed straight from the pages of George Orwell's *1984*: "From a marketing point of view," Card said, "you don't introduce new products in August."[44] The new product was introduced the following month by National Security Adviser Condoleezza Rice, who warned, "We don't want the smoking gun to be a mushroom cloud."[45] The same week, on the anniversary of 9/11, Bush declared the United States would "not allow any terrorist or tyrant to threaten civilization with weapons of mass murder."[46] The next day, in an address to the UN, Bush reiterated that Iraq was a "grave and gathering danger."[47]

On October 7, Bush invoked the 9/11 attacks and Rice's dramatic imagery: "Facing clear evidence of peril, we cannot wait for the final proof—the smoking gun — that could come in the form of a mushroom cloud." He also painted a picture of an Iraq–al-Qaeda connection linked to WMDs:

> We know that Iraq and al Qaeda have had high-level contacts that go back a decade. Some al Qaeda leaders who fled Afghanistan went to Iraq. These include one very senior al Qaeda leader who received medical treatment in Baghdad this year, and who has been associated with planning for chemical and biological attacks. We've learned that Iraq has trained al Qaeda members in bomb-making and poisons and deadly gases.

Bush declared, "We agree that the Iraqi dictator must not be permitted to threaten America and the world with horrible poisons and diseases and gases and atomic weapons."[48]

Three weeks before the midterm elections, Congress gave Bush the "Joint Resolution to Authorize the Use of United States Armed Forces Against Iraq."[49] The White House wanted to pass the resolution while many in Congress were facing reelection; those who opposed Bush's war on Iraq would be painted as "soft on terror."[50] The resolution said Iraq posed a "continuing threat to the national security of the United States" by "continuing to possess and develop a significant chemical and biological weapons capability" and "actively seeking a nuclear weapons capability."[51] It authorized the President to use the Armed Forces to "defend the national security of the United States against the continuing threat posed by Iraq" and to "enforce all relevant United Nations Security Council Resolutions regarding Iraq." Iraq didn't pose a threat to the United States, and only the UN Security Council has the power to enforce its resolutions. But Congress capitulated to the Bush gang's hyperbole and intense pressure. Some legislators later said they were duped by the Bush administration into voting for this resolution.

In his 2003 State of the Union Address, Bush famously claimed, "The British government has learned that Saddam Hussein recently sought significant quantities of uranium from Africa."[52] It was pure fiction. The White House later admitted it "should not have risen to the level of a presidential speech."[53] Bush and his officials continued to maintain the illusion of diplomacy until the day they invaded Iraq. "The White House kept saying that no decision had been made about Iraq, but only the blind or the deaf could fail to see that a decision had long ago been made," Frank Rich wrote in *The Greatest Story Ever Sold.*[54]

THE REAL MOTIVE

Why was Bush so determined to invade Iraq? Wolfowitz admitted that the WMD rationale was a "bureaucratic" excuse for war on which everyone could agree.[55] When no WMDs turned up, Wolfowitz revealed a new *raison d'etre*: the invasion of Iraq was a way to redraw the Middle East to reduce the terrorist threat to the United States.[56]

In November 2002, Rumsfeld sought to decouple oil access from regime change in Iraq when he claimed that the U.S. beef with Iraq had "nothing to do with oil, literally nothing to do with oil."[57] A year later, Bush announced in his State of the Union Address, "We have no desire to dominate, no ambitions of empire."[58] But the denials were unconvincing, and a great deal of evidence suggests that oil and domination had everything to do with the decision to invade. Indeed, while campaigning for Republican candidates during the 2006 midterm elections, in the face of calls by Democrats to withdraw from Iraq, Bush cited oil as a reason for the United States to remain in Iraq.[59]

Some of that evidence again leads back to Dick Cheney. As Defense Secretary in President George H. W. Bush's cabinet, Cheney had sponsored the 1992 draft "Pentagon Defense Planning Guidance on Post-Cold War Strategy" directed by Undersecretary of Defense Paul Wolfowitz. According to the draft, the grand objective in the Middle East and Southwest Asia was "to remain the predominant outside power in the region to preserve U.S. and Western access to the region's oil."[60] Having served as chief executive officer of the world's largest oil services company, Vice President Cheney made hegemony over the world's oil supply a foreign policy priority. In May 2001, his secret energy task force called on the White House to make "energy security a priority of U.S. trade and foreign policy" and encourage Persian Gulf countries to incorporate foreign investment in their energy sectors.[61] Later, Judicial Watch secured secret documents containing maps and plans for taking over Iraq's oil.[62]

In February 2001, a month after Bush's inauguration, White House officials discussed a memo called "Plan for Post-Saddam Iraq," which described troop requirements, establishing war crimes tribunals, and dividing up Iraq's oil wealth.[63] Meanwhile, Treasury Secretary Paul O'Neill was astonished to discover that actual plans "were already being discussed to take over Iraq and occupy it—complete with disposition of oil fields, peacekeeping forces, and war crimes tribunals—carrying forward an unspoken doctrine of preemptive war."[64] According to O'Neill, a preemptive attack on Iraq and the prospect of dividing the world's second largest oil reserve among the world's contractors "made for an irresistible combination."[65]

Bush's imperial motives are corroborated by the massive construction projects undertaken in Iraq, including an enormous American embassy in Baghdad and the largest foreign U.S. military base built since Vietnam. The new embassy occupies a space two thirds the area of the National Mall in Washington, DC. Its 21 buildings will house more than 8,000 government officials as well as a huge pool, gym, theater, beauty salon, school, and six apartment buildings. Camp Anaconda, which sits on 15 square miles of Iraqi soil near Balad, is home to 20,000 soldiers and thousands of contractors, and its air base is the second busiest in the world after Chicago's O'Hare airport. Between five and thirteen additional U.S. military bases are being built in Iraq. Bush is pushing for an Iraqi law that would give foreign companies influence over Iraq's oil. In short, the Bush administration shows no intention of leaving Iraq, suggesting that a permanent military presence is a key to the administration's real motive.

THE SELF-DEFENSE ARGUMENT

Returning to the legality of the Iraq invasion and occupation, we find that the UN Charter requires all members to settle their international disputes by peaceful means. No nation may use military force against the territorial integrity or political independence of any other country. As noted earlier, the only two exceptions to this prohibition are when a nation acts in self-defense or when the UN Security Council authorizes the use of force. A country may use military force in individual or collective self-defense "if an armed attack occurs" against a UN member country or in response to an imminent attack.[66] It is well established that the need for self-defense must be "instant, overwhelming, leaving no choice of means, and no moment for deliberation."[67]

Iraq had not attacked any other nation for 12 years. It lacked both the capacity and the will to lodge an imminent attack on any country. Its military capability had been severely weakened by the Gulf War, years of punishing sanctions and intrusive inspections, and almost daily bombing raids by the United States and Britain over the "no-fly zones."

Bush made little pretense that Iraq constituted an imminent threat. Rather, he invoked his own doctrine of "preemptive war" to justify his attack. He unveiled that doctrine in a speech at West Point in June 2002. "We must take the battle to the enemy," Bush said, "disrupt his plans, and confront the worst threats before they emerge."[68] In September of that year, he also released his National Security Strategy that purported to justify preemptive war:

> The United States has long maintained the option of preemptive actions to counter a sufficient threat to our national security. The greater the threat, the greater is the risk of inaction—and the more compelling the case for taking anticipatory action to defend ourselves, even if uncertainty remains as to the time and place of the enemy's attack. To forestall or prevent such hostile acts by our adversaries, the United States will, if necessary, act preemptively.[69]

The international community was unmoved. Quite simply, the U.S. invasion of Iraq wasn't self-defense because it didn't respond to an armed or imminent attack.

THE SECURITY COUNCIL NEVER AUTHORIZED WAR

Articles 41 and 42 of the UN Charter declare that no member has the right to enforce any Security Council resolution with military action unless the Security Council decides there has been a material breach of its resolution and all nonmilitary means of enforcement have been exhausted. Then the Council may authorize the use of military force. The use of armed force for preemptive or retaliatory purposes is incompatible with the purposes of the UN Charter and is prohibited by Article 2(4) of the charter.

The United States had been here before. In 1990, President George H. W. Bush persuaded members of the Security Council to sanction Operation Desert Storm by bribing them with cheap Saudi oil, new arms packages, and development aid.[70] In Resolution 678, the Council authorized the use of force only to expel Iraq from Kuwait.[71] Once that goal was accomplished, the authorization terminated. Since then, the Security Council has not sanctioned the use of force against Iraq. Resolution 687, passed after the Gulf War ended, required Iraq to cooperate fully with UN weapons inspectors, but the Security Council reserved to itself the power to take "such further steps as may be required for the implementation of the present resolution."[72] In 1998, the Security Council warned Iraq in Resolution 1154 of the "severest consequences" if it continued its refusal to comply. But again the Council reserved the authority to "ensure implementation of this resolution, and to secure peace and security in the area."[73]

In November 2002, the Security Council passed Resolution 1441, which established a timetable and inspections regimen in Iraq. It warned of "serious consequences" if Iraq did not comply with its requirements. But the resolution left it to the Council, not the United States, to decide what those consequences would be.[74] Indeed, China, France, and Russia—three of the five permanent members of the Security Council—issued a joint statement to clarify that point:

> Resolution 1441 (2002) adopted today by the Security Council excludes any automaticity in the use of force. . . . In case of failure by Iraq to comply with its obligations, . . . such failure

will be reported to the Security Council. . . . It will be then for
the Council to take a position on the basis of that report.[75]

But Bush was never interested in achieving a diplomatic solu-
tion in Iraq. Indeed, the Conyers report later found that Bush
sought a Security Council resolution authorizing his war simply
to provide an ultimatum that Iraq would reject.[76]

Meanwhile, the Bush administration was losing patience
with weapons inspections. Hans Blix, chief inspector of the
United Nations Monitoring, Verification and Inspection Com-
mission (UNMOVIC), recalled Cheney saying that the United
States was "ready to discredit inspections in favor of disarma-
ment."[77] And according to Bob Woodward, press reports of
Iraq's cooperation with the weapons inspectors "infuriated"
Bush, who told Rice, "The "pressure isn't holding together."[78]
The following month, Hans Blix appeared before the Security
Council and refuted Colin Powell's claims that trucks were
being used for chemical decontamination and that Iraq knew
when the weapons inspectors would be arriving. Mohamed
ElBaradei, director of the International Atomic Energy Agency,
said there was no evidence Hussein had any viable nuclear program.[79] In light of these facts, journalist Mark Danner concluded that the idea of UN inspectors was introduced "not as a
means to avoid war, as President Bush repeatedly assured Americans, but as a means to make war possible."[80]

Bush tried mightily to arrange a second Security Council resolution that would authorize his war, but the Council refused.
Bush then cobbled together prior resolutions to rationalize his
invasion. None of them, however, individually or collectively,
constituted authorization for his use of force against Iraq.

On September 15, 2004, UN Secretary General Kofi Annan
finally declared that the U.S.-led war on Iraq was illegal. Annan

told the BBC World Service, "From our point of view and from the Charter's point of view, it was illegal."[81] Hans Corell, who served as United Nations Under Secretary and Chief United Nations Legal Officer from 1994–2004, agreed with Annan. In 2006, Corell told a group of students that the U.S.–UK attack on Iraq was not carried out in self-defense or with the approval of the Security Council and thus violated the UN Charter.[82] Even neoconservative Richard Perle acknowledged that Bush's invasion of Iraq was unlawful. Perle admitted, "International law . . . would have required us to leave Saddam Hussein alone."[83]

Faced with Iraq's increasing cooperation with weapons inspectors in the weeks leading up to the invasion, Bush's rationale for disarming Iraq morphed into "regime change" to bring democracy to the Iraqi people. But forcible regime change violates the International Covenant on Civil and Political Rights (ICCPR),[84] a treaty ratified by the United States and therefore part of our domestic law under the Supremacy Clause of the Constitution.[85] Article 1(1) says: "All peoples have the right of self-determination. By virtue of that right they freely determine their political status and freely pursue their economic, social and cultural development."

The ICCPR also provides peoples with protection of their natural resources:

> All peoples may, for their own ends, freely dispose of their natural wealth and resources without prejudice to any obligations arising out of international economic cooperation, based upon the principle of mutual benefit, and international law. In no case may a people be deprived of its own means of subsistence.[86]

In a series of cases decided between 1970 and 1995, the International Court of Justice held that the principle of self-determination has become a rule of customary international law, binding on all nations.[87] The United States does not have the legal authority to intervene in the affairs of the Iraqi people and choose their leadership for them.

SHOCK AND AWE—AND THE CONSEQUENCES

Despite the absence of Security Council authorization, a quarter million troops from the United States and the United Kingdom invaded Iraq in March 2003. Delivering on their promise to "shock and awe," the "coalition forces" dropped several 2,000-pound bombs on Baghdad in rapid succession, in what the *New York Times* dubbed "almost biblical power."[88]

Since then, the use of cluster bombs, depleted uranium, and white phosphorous gas by U.S. forces in Iraq has been documented.[89] These are weapons of mass destruction. Cluster-bomb canisters contain tiny "bomblets" that can spread over a large area. Unexploded cluster bombs are frequently picked up by children and explode, resulting in serious injury or death. Depleted uranium weapons spread high levels of radiation over vast areas of land. The use of cluster bombs and depleted uranium was widely condemned by nongovernmental organizations at the 2003 session of the United Nations Commission on Human Rights. White phosphorous gas melts the skin and burns to the bone.[90] The Geneva Convention Relative to the Protection of Civilian Persons in time of War (Geneva IV) classifies "willfully causing great suffering or serious injury to body or health" as a grave breach.[91] The U.S. War Crimes Act punishes grave breaches of the Geneva Conventions as war crimes. The United States has used cluster bombs, depleted uranium, and white phosphorous gas in Iraq, weapons that cause great suffering and serious bodily injury; their use thus constitutes a grave breach. The Bush administration is committing war crimes with its use of these weapons.

"Operation Iraqi Freedom" unleashed a tragedy of immense

proportion. More than 3,000 American soldiers and tens of thousands of Iraqis have been killed. Close to 7,000 Iraqi civilians were killed in July and August 2006 alone. In October 2006, the British medical journal the *Lancet* published a study conducted by Iraqi physicians with oversight by epidemiologists at Johns Hopkins University's Bloomberg School of Public Health. The study estimated that 655,000 Iraqi civilians have died since the United States invaded Iraq in March 2003. This figure does not include Iraqis who died as a result of the punishing sanctions tht preceded the invasion.[92]

Loss of life isn't the only shocking and awful consequence of "Operation Iraqi Freedom." UN special investigator Manfred Nowak reported that torture conducted by private militias and the Iraqi government was "totally out of hand. The situation is so bad many people say it is worse than it has been in the times of Saddam Hussein."[93] The United Nations concluded in its July–August 2006 report that bodies found "often bear signs of severe torture, including acid-induced injuries and burns caused by chemical substances, missing skin, broken bones (back, hands, and legs), missing eyes, missing teeth, and wounds caused by power drills or nails."[94]

Bush's war has ignited sectarian violence and spawned a civil war. Kidnappings are widespread, and hostages are frequently killed even after their ransoms are paid. When Sunnis go to the morgue to claim the bodies of their loved ones, they are often kidnapped and killed.[95] Violence is directed at women, students, and professors, and 84 percent of the colleges have been destroyed. Amidst this violence, six in ten Iraqis polled approve of attacks on U.S.-led forces. Four in five think the U.S. military force in Iraq provokes more violence than it prevents.[96]

Furthermore, "Operation Iraqi Freedom" has led to anti-American sentiment elsewhere. According to a declassified portion of the April 2006 National Intelligence Estimate, which represents the consensus of the 16 U.S. intelligence agencies, "The Iraq conflict has become the 'cause célebrè' for jihadists, breeding a deep resentment of U.S. involvement in the Muslim world and cultivating supporters for the global jihadist movement." The report concludes, "The Iraq jihad is shaping a new generation of terrorist leaders and operatives."[97] General Pervez Musharraf of Pakistan agreed, noting on American television that the war in Iraq "has led certainly to more extremists and terrorism around the world."[98]

THE GREATEST MENACE OF OUR TIMES

The Nuremberg Charter defines *crimes against peace* as "planning, preparation, initiation or waging of a war of aggression, or a war in violation of international treaties, agreements or assurances, or participation in a common plan or conspiracy for the accomplishment of any of the foregoing."[99] Bush's war on Iraq is a war of aggression and thus constitutes a *crime against peace.*

U.S. Supreme Court Justice Robert Jackson was the chief prosecutor at the Nuremberg Tribunal. In his opening statement in 1945, Justice Jackson wrote, "No political, military, economic, or other considerations shall serve as an excuse or justification" for a war of aggression:[100]

> If certain acts in violation of treaties are crimes, they are crimes whether the United States does them or whether Germany does them, and we are not prepared to lay down a rule of criminal conduct against others which we would be unwilling to have invoked against us.[101]

Following the Holocaust, the International Military Tribunal at Nuremberg called the waging of aggressive war "essentially an evil thing. . . . To initiate a war of aggression . . . is not only an

international crime; it is the supreme international crime differ-
ing only from other war crimes in that it contains within itself
the accumulated evil of the whole."[102] Justice Jackson labeled
the crime of aggression "the greatest menace of our times."[103]
More than 50 years later, his words still ring true in Iraq.

TWO

THE TORTURE OF PRISONERS

If Bush administration officials were willing to violate the law before 9/11, they went public with that willingness after the attacks. Vice President Cheney announced on *Meet the Press* that the U.S. government might "have to work . . . sort of on the dark side."[1] Cofer Black, head of the Central Intelligence Agency (CIA) Counterterrorist Center, testified at a joint hearing of the House and Senate Intelligence Committees in September 2002, "There was a before 9/11 and an after 9/11. After 9/11, the gloves came off."[2]

These statements indirectly refer to systematic violations of U.S. and international law. Soon after 9/11, senior administration lawyers wrote memoranda to redefine and justify torture. Top intelligence and defense officials authorized interrogation techniques that rose to the level of torture as defined by international and domestic law. Brushing aside established law, President Bush announced that the Geneva Conventions didn't protect his adversaries imprisoned at Guantánamo. Later, the interrogation techniques used there were exported to Iraq, where detainees were certainly protected by those conventions. And although international law requires countries to seek out and punish torturers, the Bush gang has delivered suspected adversaries to governments with established reputations for torture.

Torture is a war crime. It violates at least two U.S. laws, the War Crimes Act of 1996 and the Torture Statute of 1994.[3] It also violates treaties we have ratified, one of which says, "No exceptional circumstances whatsoever, whether a state of war or a threat of war, internal or political instability or any other public emergency, may be invoked as a justification for torture."[4] Ever since the Nuremberg Tribunal, torturers and their commanders, all the way up to the commander in chief, have been subject to prosecution.

The first public indication that the United States would engage in torture and inhumane treatment came shortly after the invasion of Afghanistan. When John Walker Lindh was captured in December 2001, his American interrogators stripped and gagged him, strapped him to a board, and displayed him to the press while Lindh writhed in pain from a bullet in his body. Although Lindh was initially charged with crimes of terrorism carrying life in prison, former Attorney General John Ashcroft permitted him to plead guilty to lesser offenses that garnered him 20 years. The condition was that Lindh would make a statement that he suffered "no deliberate mistreatment" while in custody. The cover-up was under way. Even so, Bush reaffirmed the United States' prohibition on torture in a June 2003 press release: "The US is committed to the world-wide elimination of torture and we are leading this fight by example."[5] In a January 2005 interview with the *New York Times*, he stated that "torture is never acceptable, nor do we hand over people to countries that do torture."[6]

Yet in April 2004, the publication of grotesque photographs of torture and abuse at Iraq's Abu Ghraib prison sent shock waves around the world. Earlier reports of mistreatment had gone largely unnoticed, but images of naked prisoners stacked on one another, dogs snarling at terrified inmates, and a hooded, wired detainee perched atop a box drew outrage. Bush declared, "I shared a deep disgust that those prisoners were treated the way they were treated." He vowed the incidents would be investigated and the perpetrators "will be taken care of."[7]

Over time, the treatment of prisoners in Iraq, Afghanistan, Guantánamo, and secret CIA "black sites" around the world spoke louder than Bush's declaration to lead the fight against torture by example. In its 2005 report, for example, the bipartisan 9/11 Commission concluded, "The U.S. policy on treating detainees is undermining the war on terrorism by tarnishing America's reputation as a moral leader."[8] Britain's House of Commons, the UN Secretary-General, the UN Special Rapporteurs on Torture and Arbitrary Detention, and the Inter-American Commission on Human Rights have all concluded that the U.S. treatment of prisoners violates international law.[9]

A few low-ranking soldiers and a chief warrant officer have been tried for criminal offenses, but no prosecutions have been initiated under the Torture Convention Implementation Act or the War Crimes Act, and no high-level officials have been prosecuted for violations of criminal law. Moreover, military defense lawyers who vigorously represent their clients have been threatened with punishment or passed over for promotion. After Lt. Col. Colby Vokey and Sgt. Heather Cerveny reported allegations of prisoner abuse at Guantánamo in October 2006, the Marine Corps imposed a gag order on them and threatened to punish them for speaking out.[10] The Navy command denied a promotion for Salim Ahmed Hamdan's lawyer, Lt. Cmdr. Charles Swift, two weeks after he won his client's case in the Supreme Court. Three other military defense attorneys met the same fate as Swift.[11]

U.S. AND INTERNATIONAL LAWS
AGAINST TORTURE

Laws prohibiting torture are clear and consistent. In 1994, the United States ratified the Convention Against Torture and Other Cruel, Inhuman or Degrading Treatment or Punishment and thereby prohibited the intentional infliction of severe physical or mental pain or suffering to obtain a confession, punish, intimidate, or coerce a detainee for any reason.[12] The Torture Convention also requires each party to "undertake to prevent in any territory under its jurisdiction other acts of cruel, inhuman or degrading treatment or punishment which do not amount to torture." In other words, the convention sought to prevent all mistreatment, not just torture. When Congress subsequently passed the Torture Convention Implementation Act, it authorized individual criminal liability as well as penalties up to and including death.

The United States is also a party to the International Covenant on Civil and Political Rights (ICCPR). By ratifying the ICCPR, the United States prohibited torture as well as cruel, inhuman, or degrading treatment; guaranteed the right to life; and stipulated that these rights cannot be weakened or diminished, even during a public emergency or armed conflict threatening the life of a nation. In other words, our government is *never* permitted to torture or abuse prisoners.

Perhaps the most famous anti-torture treaties are the four Geneva Conventions, which the United States ratified in 1955. The first two provide for the protection of sick and wounded soldiers and sailors on the field of battle. The third convention sets forth criteria to determine who is a prisoner of war (POW) and establishes minimum standards for treatment of POWs. When doubt arises about a person's POW status, a competent tribunal must decide it. In the meantime, the prisoner must be afforded the protections of this convention, which include being treated humanely at all times. POWs must be protected against violence to life and person, intimidation, mutilation, and outrages upon personal dignity, particularly humiliating and degrading treatment. No physical or mental torture, or any other form of coercion, may be inflicted on POWs to obtain information of any kind whatsoever. Those who refuse to answer questions may not be threatened, insulted, or exposed to any unpleasant or disadvantageous treatment. POWs need only provide their surnames, first names, rank, date of birth, and serial number.

The fourth convention pertains to protection of civilians during wartime and requires that protected persons, including detainees, be treated humanely. Again, they must be shielded from violence to life and person, intimidation, mutilation, and outrages on personal dignity, particularly humiliating and degrading treatment. No physical or moral coercion can be used against them to obtain information from them.

When any country ratifies these conventions, it agrees to search for persons who have committed or ordered the commission of grave breaches of the conventions. Grave breaches include willful killing, torture or inhuman treatment and willfully causing great suffering or serious injury to body or health. Such countries must then either bring those persons before their own courts or transfer them to another party for trial.

All four conventions contain an identical article, often referred to as Common Article Three. It requires that persons taking no active part in hostilities, including those under detention, be treated humanely at all times. They must be protected against violence to life and person, particularly murder, mutilation, cruel treatment, and torture; hostage-taking; and outrages upon personal dignity, particularly humiliating and degrading treatment.

Forty-one years after the United States became a party to the Geneva Conventions, a Republican Congress passed a federal criminal statute to implement our obligations under its provisions. The War Crimes Act of 1996 provides for fines, life imprisonment, or even death for someone who commits a war crime, whether inside or outside the United States. War crimes under this act include grave breaches of the Geneva Conventions and violations of Common Article Three. Thus, murder, torture, and cruel or inhuman treatment can be punished under this statute.

Until the Supreme Court decided *Hamdan v. Rumsfeld* in June 2006, the Bush administration took the position that Common Article Three didn't cover al-Qaeda prisoners. In *Hamdan*, the Supreme Court found otherwise and referred to possible criminal liability under the War Crimes Act. The Bush administration mounted a full-court press to amend the War Crimes Act, and Congress complied by passing the Military Commissions Act of 2006. That act removed "outrages upon personal dignity, particularly humiliating and degrading treatment" from the list of offenses punishable by the War Crimes Act. The new law also immunizes administration officials from war crimes prosecutions for past torture and abuse of prisoners in U.S. custody.

THE TORTURE MEMOS

How did the United States find itself on the wrong side of torture prohibitions? Some of the most disturbing documentary evidence starts with the January 2002 memo from White House Counsel Alberto Gonzales to Bush:

> As you said, the war against terrorism is a new kind of war. It is not the traditional clash between nations adhering to the laws of war that formed the backdrop for the GPW [Geneva

III]. The nature of the new war places a high premium on other factors, such as the ability to quickly obtain information from captured terrorists and their sponsors in order to avoid further atrocities against American civilians, and the need to try terrorists for war crimes such as wantonly killing civilians.

Thus, Gonzales concluded, "This new paradigm renders obsolete Geneva's strict limitation on questioning of enemy prisoners and renders quaint some of its provisions."[13]

Concerned about prosecution under the War Crimes Act, Gonzales advised Bush to declare that Geneva didn't apply to the war against the Taliban and al-Qaeda in Afghanistan: "Your determination [to bypass the Geneva Conventions] would create a reasonable basis in law that Section 2441 [the War Crimes Statute] does not apply, which would provide a solid defense to any future [war crimes] prosecution." But when Secretary of State Colin Powell saw Gonzales's memo, he reportedly "hit the roof."[14] Powell wrote to Gonzales and National Security Adviser Condoleezza Rice, warning that Gonzales's plan "will reverse over a century of U.S. policy and practice in supporting the Geneva conventions, and undermine the protection of the law of war for our troops, both in this specific conflict and in general."[15]

Bush ignored Powell's warning. On February 7, 2002, he announced that detainees from Afghanistan were ineligible for hearings to decide their POW status and that Common Article Three of Geneva didn't apply to them.[16] He then declared, "As a matter of policy, the United States Armed Forces shall continue to treat detainees humanely and, to the extent appropriate and consistent with military necessity, in a manner consistent with the principles of Geneva." As a matter of U.S. law, however, the government is required to treat all detainees humanely at *all* times.

In response to a request from Gonzales, John Yoo and Jay
Bybee, writing for the Department of Justice's (DOJ) Office of
Legal Counsel (OLC), advised in an August 2002 memo that
interrogators who torture al-Qaeda or Taliban prisoners could
be exempt from torture prosecutions under the President's
commander-in-chief powers.[17] But the Torture Convention permits no such exemption, even during wartime. Perhaps most
alarming was the memo's narrowing of the definitions of torture
that had long been in use. It argued that severe physical suffering
caused by acts of torture "must be equivalent in intensity to the
pain accompanying serious physical injury, such as organ failure,
impairment of bodily function, or even death." Severe mental
suffering "must penetrate to the core of an individual's ability to
perceive the world around him, substantially interfering with his
cognitive abilities, or fundamentally alter his personality." Yoo
and Bybee wrote that psychological harm must last "months or
even years" to amount to torture. Finally, the OLC memo
opined that self-defense or necessity could provide defenses to
war crimes prosecutions, again in spite of the Torture Convention's absolute prohibition on torture. A similar "lesser evil" defense was rejected at Nuremberg and in later occupation trials.[18]

When the OLC memo leaked, the White House quickly dis-
avowed it as the work of a small group of Justice Department lawyers. According to *Newsweek,* however, the memo was
drafted after Gonzales met with Defense Department General
Counsel William Haynes and David Addington, Vice President
Cheney's counsel, to discuss specific interrogation techniques.[19]
In an effort to control the damage, the Justice Department issued a new memo in December 2004 that redefined torture
more broadly and admitted that a defendant's national security
motives did not shield him from a torture prosecution.

During the January 2005 Senate hearings to confirm him as

Attorney General, Gonzales was asked whether the President could ignore the ban on torture. He replied, "I guess I would have to say that hypothetically that authority may exist."[20] Yoo continues to be one of the Bush gang's primary advisors. He was the architect of the Patriot Act and the domestic surveillance program. Bybee was later appointed to the U.S. Court of Appeals for the Ninth Circuit.

THE RUMSFELD FACTOR

Once the lawyers had done their work, the Pentagon weighed in. Throughout the summer and fall of 2002, harsh interrogations were conducted at Guantánamo. According to journalist Seymour Hersh, a CIA analyst was sent there in late summer to find out why so little useful intelligence had been gathered. After interviewing 30 prisoners, Hersh wrote, "He came back convinced that we were committing war crimes in Guantánamo."[21]

During the fall, Donald Rumsfeld received updates on the interrogation of a Saudi detainee, Mohamed al-Qahtani, at Guantánamo. Major General Geoffrey Miller, who later transferred many of his interrogation techniques to Abu Ghraib, supervised the interrogation and reported to Rumsfeld weekly. Over a six-week period, al-Qahtani was stripped naked, forced to wear women's underwear on his head, denied bathroom access, threatened with dogs, forced to perform tricks while tethered to a dog leash, and subjected to sleep deprivation.[22] He was also kept in solitary confinement for 160 days and interrogated for 18 to 20 hours a day for 48 days during one 54-day period.[23]

In December 2002, Rumsfeld approved interrogation techniques that included the use of dogs, hooding, stress positions, isolation for up to 30 days, 20-hour interrogations, deprivation of light and sound, using "scenarios to convince the detainee that death or severely painful consequences are imminent for him and/or his family," and using "a wet towel and dripping water to induce the misperception of suffocation."[24]

After U.S. Navy General Counsel Alberto J. Mora learned that "coercive interrogation techniques . . . had been reportedly authorized at a high level in Washington," he met with William Haynes, the Pentagon's general counsel, on December 20, 2002.[25] Mora told Haynes that Rumsfeld's "authorized interrogation techniques could rise to the level of torture." When Mora prepared a draft memorandum critical of these techniques, the Pentagon backed down. On January 15, 2003, Rumsfeld rescinded his general approval of some techniques but left open the possibility that he would approve them on a case-by-case basis.[26] One of the techniques Rumsfeld reserved the right to allow was water-boarding.[27] An Army investigation later found that by mid-October 2003, "interrogation policy in Iraq had changed three times in less than thirty days and it became very confusing as to what techniques could be employed and at what level non-doctrinal approaches had to be approved"[28]

In May 2004, Rumsfeld told a Senate Committee investigating abuses in Iraq and Guantánamo that the Geneva Conventions apply to all detainees in Iraq; however, he maintained that the protections didn't apply to prisoners at Guantánamo because they were all "terrorists."[29] Yet even in Iraq, the Bush administration tried to deny Geneva protections to some prisoners by transferring them to other countries.[30] *Newsweek* reported that Bush "authorized the CIA to set up a series of secret detention facilities outside the United States and to question those held in them with unprecedented harshness."[31] The Bush administration refused to confirm the existence of these infamous "black sites" until September 2006, when Bush announced the transfer of Khalid Sheikh Mohammed and 13 other alleged terrorists from these CIA prisons to Guantánamo.

Even within Iraq, however, the evidence is damning. In a September 2005 report, Human Rights Watch documented the reports of Army Captain Ian Fishback and two sergeants from the 82nd Airborne Division who were responsible for supervising prisoners in Iraq. The torture and other mistreatment of Iraqis in detention were "systematic and was known at varying levels of command."[32] The report went on to recount the soldiers' testimony:

> The acts of torture and other cruel or inhuman treatment they described include severe beatings (in one incident, a soldier reportedly broke a detainee's leg with a baseball bat), blows and kicks to the face, chest, abdomen, and extremities, and repeated kicks to various parts of the detainees' body; the application of chemical substances to exposed skin and eyes; forced stress positions, such as holding heavy water jugs with arms outstretched, sometimes to the point of unconsciousness; sleep deprivation; subjecting detainees to extremes of hot and cold; the stacking of detainees into human pyramids; and, the withholding of food (beyond crackers) and water.[33]

After Captain Fishback reported to the Senate Armed Services Committee, Senator John McCain garnered overwhelming support in both houses of Congress for a law clarifying that the United States will not subject prisoners in its custody to cruel, inhuman, or degrading treatment or punishment, regardless of geographic location. Cheney unsuccessfully lobbied McCain to provide an exemption for the CIA. Bush finally signed the bill but attached a "signing statement," declaring that his administration would interpret the new law to his own liking.[34]

On November 3, 2005, the Department of Defense issued a new policy on military interrogations that barred torture and called for the humane treatment of detainees. However, it contained a loophole that would allow the secretary of defense or deputy secretary of defense to override the policy.[35]

THE HUMAN CONSEQUENCES

One of the first victims of the Bush administration's 2002 torture policy was Abu Zubaydah. Captured in April of that year, Zubaydah was characterized as the "chief of operations" for al-Qaeda and bin Laden's "number three" man. The Bush administration tortured him repeatedly at the CIA "black sites." They water-boarded him, withheld his medication, threatened him with impending death, and bombarded him with continuous deafening noise and harsh lights.

But Zubaydah wasn't a top al-Qaeda leader. Dan Coleman, one of the Federal Bureau of Investigation's (FBI's) leading experts on al-Qaeda, said of Zubaydah, "He knew very little about real operations, or strategy. . . . He was expendable, you know, the greeter . . . Joe Louis in the lobby of Caeser's Palace, shaking hands." Moreover, Zubaydah was schizophrenic; according to Coleman, "This guy is insane, certifiable split personality." Coleman's views were seconded at the top levels of the CIA and were communicated to Bush and Cheney. But Bush scolded CIA director George Tenet, saying, "I said [Zubaydah] was important. You're not going to let me lose face on this, are you?" Zubaydah's minor role in al-Qaeda and his apparent insanity were kept secret.[36]

In response to the torture, Zubaydah told his interrogators about myriad terrorist targets al-Qaeda had in its sights: the Brooklyn Bridge, the Statute of Liberty, shopping malls, banks, supermarkets, water systems, nuclear plants, and apartment buildings and reported that al-Qaeda was close to building a crude nuclear bomb. None of this was corroborated, but the Bush gang reacted to each report zealously.[37]

In February 2004, the International Committee of the Red Cross (ICRC) issued a report documenting the treatment of prisoners by Coalition Forces in Iraq.[38] It concluded that detainees "were at high risk of being subjected to a variety of harsh treatments" that were "tantamount to torture." Furthermore, the ICRC reported, military intelligence officers told the ICRC that between 70% and 90% of the persons detained had been arrested by mistake. The methods of ill treatment most frequently alleged during interrogation included hooding, sometimes in conjunction with beatings, for up to four consecutive days; threats of ill treatment, reprisals against family members, imminent execution, or transfer to Guantánamo; stripping prisoners naked for several days in an empty, dark cell; depriving them of sleep, food, or water; parading them naked before other prisoners and laughing guards, some of them female; handcuffing them to the bars of their cell door in humiliating or uncomfortable positions; exposing them while hooded to loud noise, music, or intense heat, including weather up to 122° F; and forcing them to remain in stress positions, such as squatting or standing with arms lifted, for prolonged periods.

On January 31, 2004, Major General Antonio W. Taguba was appointed to investigate the activities of the 800th Military Police Brigade at Abu Ghraib. His report determined that "between October and December 2003, at the Abu Ghraib Confinement Facility (BCCF), numerous incidents of sadistic, blatant, and wanton criminal abuses were inflicted on several detainees. This systematic and illegal abuse of detainees was intentionally perpetrated by several members of the military police guard force."[39] Taguba found that military police punched, slapped, and kicked detainees; forcibly arranged them in sexually explicit positions for photographing; kept detainees naked for several days at a time; forced naked male detainees to wear women's underwear; forced groups of male detainees to masturbate while being photographed and videotaped; arranged naked male detainees in a pile and jumped on them; positioned a naked detainee on a box with a sandbag on his head and attached wires to his fingers, toes, and penis to simulate electric torture; used military working dogs without muzzles to intimidate and frighten detainees; and sodomized a detainee with a chemical light and perhaps a broomstick.[40] Taguba concluded, "Several US Army Soldiers have committed egregious acts and grave breaches of international law at Abu Ghraib/BCCF and Camp Bucca, Iraq."[41]

In August 2004, the Independent Panel to Review Department of Defense Detention Operations issued its report, also known as the Schlesinger Report. It concluded that "Policies approved for use on al Qaeda and Taliban detainees, who were not afforded the protection of the Geneva Conventions, now applied to detainees who did fall under the Geneva Convention protections."[42] Another Army report released in August 2004 also determined that the most extreme abuses "are, without question, criminal."[43]

Force-Feeding Detainees

The 53-nation UN Human Rights Commission reported in February 2006 that the violent force-feeding of detainees by the U.S. military at its Guantánamo prison camp amounts to torture.[44] More than a third of the prisoners held there have refused food to protest being held incommunicado for years with no hope of release.[45] Attorney Julia Tarver's client Abdul-Rahman told her "of his determination to die and said that, 'now, after four years in captivity, life and death are the same,'" Tarver wrote in a sworn declaration filed in federal district court.[46]

Yousef Al Shehri, another of Tarver's clients, was taken prisoner by the U.S. military while he was still a juvenile. Both clients described being force-fed by the guards. Tarver wrote in her declaration:

> Yousef was the second detainee to have an NG [nasal gastric] tube inserted into his nose and pushed all the way down his throat and into his stomach, a procedure which caused him great pain. Yousef was given no anesthesia or sedative for the procedure; instead, two soldiers restrained him—one holding his chin while the other held him back by his hair, and a medical staff member forcefully inserted the tube in his nose and down his throat. Much blood came out of his nose. Yousef said he could not speak for two days after the procedure; he said he felt like a piece of metal was inside of him. He said he could not sleep because of the severe pain.

When Yousef and others "vomited up blood, the soldiers mocked and cursed at them, and taunted them with statements like 'Look what your religion has brought you,'" Tarver wrote. After two weeks of this treatment, the forced feeding stopped for five days. Then guards began to insert larger, thicker tubes into the detainees' noses. "These large tubes," Tarver wrote, "the thickness of a finger, [Yousef] estimated—were viewed by the detainees as objects of torture. They were forcibly shoved up the detainees' noses and down into their stomachs. Again, no anesthesia or sedative was provided to alleviate the obvious trauma of the procedure. . . . When the tube was removed, it was even more painful, and blood came gushing out of him. He fainted, and several of the other detainees also lost consciousness. . . . They were told that this tube would be inserted and removed twice a day every day until the hunger strike ended. Yousef described the pain as 'unbearable.'"

Both of Tarver's clients independently identified physicians as participants in this procedure. "The guards took NG tubes from one detainee, and with no sanitization whatsoever, re-inserted it into the nose of a different detainee. When these tubes were re-inserted, the detainees could see the blood and stomach bile from other detainees remaining on the tubes," Tarver wrote in her declaration.

The UN commission confirmed that "doctors and other health professionals are participating in force-feeding detainees." It cited the Declarations of Tokyo and Malta, the World Medical Association, and the American Medical Association, which prohibit doctors from participating in force-feeding a detainee, provided the detainee is capable of understanding the consequences of refusing food.[47] Red Cross guidelines state, "Doctors should never be party to actual coercive feeding. Such actions can be considered a form of torture and under no circumstances should doctors participate in them on the pretext of saving the hunger striker's life."[48]

The commission called on the U.S. government to ensure that the authorities at Guantánamo Bay do not force-feed any detainee who is capable of forming a rational judgment and is aware of the consequences of refusing food. "The United States Government should invite independent health professionals to monitor hunger strikers, in a manner consistent with international ethical standards, throughout the hunger strike," the commission proposed. It also recommended that the U.S. government "close the Guantánamo Bay detention facilities without further delay. Until the closure, and possible transfer of detainees to pretrial detention facilities on U.S. territory, the Government should refrain from any practice amounting to torture or cruel, inhuman or degrading treatment or punishment." The commission further said, "the United States Government should ensure that all allegations of torture or cruel, inhuman or degrading treatment or punishment are thoroughly investigated by an independent authority, and that all persons found to have perpetrated, ordered, tolerated or condoned such practices, up to the highest level of military and political command, are brought to justice."[49]

Not surprisingly, the Bush administration rejected the commission's report, saying that the rapporteurs who prepared the report had not visited the Guantánamo prison. The commission relied on interviews with former detainees, public documents, media reports, lawyers, and questions answered by the U.S. government. The Bush administration invited the rapporteurs to visit the prison camp but refused to allow them to speak with the prisoners. Of the more than 750 men and boys who have been detained at Guantánamo, only nine were designated for trial on criminal charges as of the end of December 2005.[50]

Torture by Proxy

The Bush administration also engages in the illegal practice of *extraordinary rendition,* where people are sent to other countries to be tortured.[51] An FBI supervisory special agent warned his superiors in a leaked November 2002 memo that extraordinary rendition was illegal. The purpose of rendition, he explained, was "to utilize, outside the U.S., interrogation techniques that would violate" federal laws against torture. The agent cautioned that extraordinary rendition would constitute a federal crime and those who planned it could be charged with conspiracy to commit torture.[52] Indeed, the Convention against Torture prohibits *refoulement*—expelling, returning, or extraditing a person to another country where there are substantial grounds to believe he would be in danger of being tortured.[53]

The head of the Council of Europe said in a January 2006 report that the United States flew detainees to countries where they would be tortured, and European governments probably knew about it. "There is a great deal of coherent, convergent evidence pointing to the existence of a system of 'relocation' or 'outsourcing' of torture," Swiss senator Dick Marty told the 46-nation Council. He estimated that more than 100 people had been subjected to rendition.[54]

In such cases, suspects are typically blindfolded, shackled, sedated, and then flown to another country, where they are often tortured and sometimes killed. Popular destinations include Egypt, Syria, Saudi Arabia, Jordan, Pakistan, Uzbekistan, and Morocco. A former CIA agent observed, "If you want a serious interrogation, you send a prisoner to Jordan. If you want them to be tortured, you send them to Syria. If you want someone to disappear—never to see them again—you send them to Egypt."[55] As of March 2005, the CIA had engaged in 100 to 150 cases of extraordinary rendition.[56]

For example, a U.S. government-leased plane transported two Egyptians from Sweden to Egypt, where they were subjected to repeated torture by electrical shocks.[57] In another case, Maher Arar, a Canadian engineer born in Syria, was apprehended in New York and sent back to Syria, where he suffered months of brutal interrogation and torture. Arar described his experience with an Arabic expression. He said the pain was so unbearable that "you forget the milk that you have been fed from the breast of your mother."[58] In September 2006, a Canadian government commission exonerated Arar of any terrorist ties.[59] Others like Arar who have been kidnapped and tortured will have no legal recourse under the Military Commissions Act of 2006.

In June 2005, an Italian judge ordered the arrest of 13 CIA operatives for the kidnapping of an Egyptian imam from the streets of Milan, who was taken to Cairo and tortured. "Kidnapping Abu Omar was not only a crime against the state of Italy, but also it did great damage to the war on terrorism," the Italian prosecutor said. "We could have continued the investigation and found evidence on other people. He would be on trial by now instead of missing."[60]

On January 31, 2007, a German court issued an arrest warrant for 13 people who were allegedly part of a CIA "abduction team" that seized Khaled el-Masri, a German citizen of Lebanese descent, in Macedonia and flew him to Afghanistan, where he was shackled, beaten, and interrogated, and then released without charges.[61]

Alberto Gonzales said that the U.S. State Department and CIA receive assurances that prisoners will be treated humanely, but he admitted, "We can't fully control what that country might do. We obviously expect a country to whom we have rendered a detainee to comply with their representations to us. . . . If you're asking me, 'Does a country always comply?' I don't have an answer to that."[62]

THE SLIPPERY SLOPE

Alberto Mora, former general counsel of the U.S. Navy, told Jane Mayer of *The New Yorker*, "To my mind, there's no moral or practical distinction" between the authorization of torture and of cruel treatment.

> If cruelty is no longer declared unlawful, but instead is applied as a matter of policy, it alters the fundamental relationship of man to government. It destroys the whole notion of individual rights. The Constitution recognizes that man has an inherent right, not bestowed by the state or laws, to personal dignity, including the right to be free of cruelty. It applies to all human beings, not just in America—even those designated "unlawful enemy combatants." If you make this exception, the whole Constitution crumbles. It's a transformative issue.[63]

The continuum from torture to inhuman and degrading treatment is a seamless one. Once some inhumane treatment is allowed, it can quickly turn into torture.

Moreover, as the U.S. Supreme Court has recognized, torture is generally ineffective for securing reliable information.[64] The Army Field Manual concurs:

> Experience indicates that the use of prohibited techniques is not necessary to gain the cooperation of interrogation sources. Use of torture and other illegal methods is a poor technique that yields unreliable results, may damage subsequent collection efforts, and can induce the source to say whatever he thinks the interrogator wants to hear.

The Army Field Manual also states that the use of torture by U.S. forces will adversely affect our own forces:

> Revelation of the use of torture by U.S. personnel will bring discredit upon the U.S. and its armed forces while undermining domestic and international support for the war effort. It may also place U.S. and allied personnel in enemy hands at greater risk of abuse by their captors.

Finally, two wrongs don't make a right, according to the Army Field Manual:

> Conversely, knowing the enemy has abused U.S. and allied PWs [prisoners of war] does not justify using methods of interrogation prohibited by the GWS [Geneva Convention on Wounded and Sick], GPW [Geneva Convention on Prisoners of War] or GC [Geneva Convention Relative to the Protection of Civilian Persons], and U.S. policy.[65]

"Brutalization doesn't work," said former FBI agent Dan Coleman. "Besides that," he added, "you lose your soul."[66] If we stand by and permit our high government officials to torture with impunity, we, too, will have lost our souls.

THREE

-)|(——)|(——)|(-

SUMMARY EXECUTION
AND WILLFUL KILLING

On November 3, 2002, an unmanned CIA surveillance aircraft killed six men in Yemen. The Bush administration, pleased with the attack, declared that the men were suspected al-Qaeda operatives.[1] Deputy Defense Secretary Paul Wolfowitz described the assassination as a "very successful tactical operation."[2] Yemen had not attacked the United States, we were not at war with Yemen, and the Security Council had not assented to this assault. Although the attack violated international and U.S. law, the legality of the hit received little media attention.

Three months later, in his January 2003 State of the Union address, Bush said, "All told, more than 3,000 suspected terrorists have been arrested in many countries. Many others have met a different fate." He added, "Let's put it this way—they are no longer a problem to the United States and our friends and allies."[3] The implication was that the U.S. government had sanctioned summary execution, in direct violation of the law.

Targeted or political assassinations—sometimes called *extrajudicial executions*—are carried out by order of, or with the acquiescence of, a government, outside any judicial framework. As a 1998 report from the UN Special Rapporteur noted, "Extra-judicial executions can never be justified under any circum-stances, not even in time of war."[4] Willful killing is a grave breach of the Geneva Conventions, punishable as a war crime under the U.S. War Crimes Act. Extrajudicial executions also vi-olate a longstanding U.S. policy. In the 1970s, after the Senate Select Committee on Intelligence disclosed that the CIA had been involved in several murders or attempted murders of for-eign leaders, President Gerald Ford issued an executive order banning assassinations. Although there have been exceptions to this policy, every succeeding president has reaffirmed that order.

The Bush administration has violated these laws and policies. Indeed, the administration's media efforts have explicitly and implicitly acknowledged the violations. Shortly after 9/11, for example, former White House press secretary Ari Fleischer in-vited the killing of Saddam Hussein. "The cost of one bullet, if the Iraqi people take it on themselves, is substantially less" than the cost of war, Fleischer said.[5]

Only later did Americans learn that Fleischer's comment reflected a secret order Bush signed in December 2001 revoking the policy begun by President Ford. That order reads in part, "The Bush administration has concluded that executive orders banning assassination do not prevent the president from law-fully singling out a terrorist for death by covert action."[6] Once again, Bush dispensed with the bedrock due process principles of the presumption of innocence and the right to a fair trial. Instead, his Presidential Finding established a "special-access program" authorizing clandestine Special Forces to snatch or as-sassinate anyone considered a "high-value" al-Qaeda operative, anywhere in the world.[7]

The Bush policy would have shocked American consciences even in the immediate aftermath of the bloodiest war in history.

As Justice Robert Jackson, chief prosecutor at the Nuremberg Tribunal, explained to President Harry Truman, "We could execute or otherwise punish [the Nazi officials] without a hearing. But undiscriminating executions or punishments without definite findings of guilt, fairly arrived at, would . . . not set easily on the American conscience or be remembered by our children with pride."[8] The U.S. government opposed the summary execution of Nazi and Japanese leaders who were charged with the most heinous crimes—genocide, war crimes, crimes against humanity, and the crime of aggression. In his opening statement at Nuremberg, Jackson said, "That four great nations, flushed with victory and stung with injury stay the hand of vengeance and voluntarily submit their captive enemies to the judgment of law is one of the most significant tributes that power has ever paid to reason."[9] He understood that the President cannot be judge, jury, and executioner.

RULES OF ENGAGEMENT, FREE-FIRE ZONES, AND CIVILIAN DEATHS

In addition to carrying out illegal assassinations, the Bush administration has set rules of engagement that have resulted in the willful killing and indiscriminate slaughter of civilians. In particular, U.S. troops in Iraq have operated in "free-fire zones," with orders to shoot everything that moves. Bombings of civilian areas and the use of depleted uranium, cluster bombs, and white phosphorous gas have resulted in massive civilian casualties, which the Bush gang casually calls "collateral damage."

The best-known free-fire zone has been Fallujah. In April 2004, four Blackwater Security Consulting mercenaries were killed in Fallujah, and their bodies were mutilated. In retaliation, U.S. forces attacked the village and killed 736 people. At least 60% of them were women and children, according to independent journalist Dahr Jamail, who interviewed doctors at Fallujah General Hospital and at other small clinics inside the city both during and after the April siege. In November 2004, NBC News correspondent Kevin Sites, embedded with the U.S. Marines, heard Staff Sgt. Sam Mortimer radio that "everything to the west is weapons free." *Weapons free,* explained Sites, "means the Marines can shoot whatever they see—it's all considered hostile."[10]

Collective punishment against an occupied population constitutes a violation of the Fourth Geneva Convention.[11] Yet according to the Study Centre for Human Rights and Democracy, the U.S. attack on Fallujah in November 2004 killed between 4,000 and 6,000 civilians.[12] During the assault, Associated Press photographer Bilal Hussein saw American soldiers "open fire on the houses" and U.S. helicopters fire on and kill people, including a family of five, who tried to cross the river.[13] "A large number of people including children were killed by American snipers," and civilians who remained in Fallujah "appeared to have been seen as complicit in the insurgency," the *Independent* (UK) reported. "Men of military age were particularly vulnerable. But there are accounts of children as young as four, and women and old men being killed."[14] Some U.S. service personnel expressed regret over the action in Fallujah. Army Captain Paul Fowler of the 1st Infantry Division said, "I really hate that it had to be destroyed. But that was the only way to root these guys out. . . . The only way to root them out is to destroy everything in your path."[15]

Like other grave breaches of the Geneva Conventions, these acts are punishable under the U.S. War Crimes Act. Commanders have a responsibility to make sure civilians are not indiscriminately harmed and that prisoners are not summarily executed. Because rules of engagement are set at the top of the command chain, criminal liability extends beyond the perpetrator under the doctrine of *command responsibility.*

Perhaps the most notable incident from the grueling urban warfare in Fallujah was captured on videotape on November 13, 2004, when Sites filmed a Marine killing an unarmed and wounded Iraqi in a Fallujah mosque. The Marine who killed the wounded Iraqi had reportedly been shot in the face himself the day before. When Sites saw the Marine shoot the unarmed, wounded man, he reported, "I feel the deep pit of my stomach." Sites told the lieutenant "that this man—all of these wounded men—were the same ones from yesterday. That they had been disarmed, treated and left here. At that point," Sites noted, "the Marine who fired the shot became aware that I was in the room. He came up to me and said, 'I didn't know sir—I didn't know.' The anger that seemed present just moments before turned to fear and dread."[16]

After Sites's report became public, there was a great outcry. Interim Iraqi Prime Minister Ayad Allawi said he was "very concerned" about the fatal shooting. UN High Commissioner for Human Rights Louise Arbour called for an investigation of allegations of the disproportionate use of force and the targeting of civilians in Fallujah. Clips from Sites's videotape were seen around the world and aired repeatedly on Al-Jazeera television. The First Marine Expeditionary Force initiated an investigation "to determine whether the Marine acted in self-defense, violated military law or failed to comply with the law of armed conflict [Geneva Convention]."[17]

The incident and its aftermath were a major story, and the existence of videotape was a contributing factor. Yet the media have largely missed the much more significant story of war crimes on a grander scale. Those crimes include, but are by no means limited to, the Haditha Massacre of 2005.

THE HADITHA MASSACRE

They ranged from little babies to adult males and
females. I'll never be able to get that out of my head.
I can still smell the blood. This left something in my
head and heart.   —Lance Cpl. Roel Ryan Briones[18]

On November 19, 2005, one year after they fought in Fallujah,
Marines from Kilo Company killed 24 unarmed civilians in
Haditha, Iraq, "execution-style," in a three- to five-hour ram-
page.[19] One victim was a 76-year-old amputee in a wheelchair
holding a Koran. A mother and child bent over as if in prayer
were also among the fallen. "I pretended that I was dead when
my brother's body fell on me and he was bleeding like a faucet,"
said Safa Younis Salim, a 13-year-old girl who survived by faking
her death.[20] Other victims included six children ranging in age
from 1 to 14.[21] Citing doctors at Haditha's hospital, the *Washington Post* reported, "Most of the shots . . . were fired at such
close range that they went through the bodies of the family
members and plowed into walls or the floor."[22]

The executions of 24 unarmed civilians were apparent retaliation for the death of Lance Cpl. Miguel [T. J.] Terrazas when a
small Marine convoy hit a roadside bomb earlier that day. A
statement issued by a U.S. Marine Corps spokesman the next
day claimed: "A U.S. Marine and 15 civilians were killed yesterday from the blast of a roadside bomb in Haditha. Immediately
following the bombing, gunmen attacked the convoy with
small-arms fire. Iraqi army soldiers and Marines returned fire,
killing eight insurgents and wounding another."[23] A subsequent
Marine version of the events said the victims were killed in-
advertently in a running gun battle with insurgents.

Both stories were false, and the Marines knew it. They were
blatant attempts to cover up the atrocity, disguised as "collateral

damage." The Marine Corps paid $38,000 in compensation to relatives of the victims according to a report in the *Denver Post*. These types of payments are made only to compensate for accidental deaths inflicted by U.S. troops. This was a relatively large amount, indicating the Marines knew something was not right during that operation, according to Mike Coffman, the Colorado state treasurer who served in Iraq recently as a Marine reservist.[24] In effect, the compensation was hush money.

Congressman John Murtha, a former Marine, was briefed on the Haditha investigation by Marine Corps Commandant Michael Hagee. Murtha said, "The reports I have from the highest level: No firing at all. No interaction. No military action at all in this particular incident. It was an explosive device, which killed a Marine. From then on, it was purely shooting people."[25] Marine Corps officials told Murtha that troops shot a woman "in cold blood" as she was bending over her child begging for mercy.[26]

The Haditha massacre did not become public until *Time* magazine ran a story in March 2006. *Time* had turned over the results of its investigation, including a videotape, to the U.S. military in January. Only then did the military launch an investigation. These Marines "suffered a total breakdown in morality and leadership, with tragic results," a U.S. official told the *Los Angeles Times*.[27]

Murtha said, "Our troops overreacted because of the pressure on them, and they killed innocent civilians in cold blood."[28] Murtha's statement both indicts and exonerates the Marines of the crime of murder. Murder is the unlawful killing of a human being with malice aforethought. Premeditation and deliberation—cold-blooded planning—are required for first-degree murder. Complete self-defense can be demonstrated by an honest and reasonable belief in the need to defend oneself against death or great bodily injury. The Marines might be able to show that, in the wake of the killing of their buddy Terrazas by an improvised explosive device, they acted in an honest belief that they might be killed in this hostile area. But the belief that unarmed civilians inside their homes posed a deadly threat to the Marines would be unreasonable. An honest but unreasonable belief in the need to defend constitutes imperfect self-defense, which negates the malice required for murder, and reduces murder to manslaughter.

Many of our troops suffer from posttraumatic stress disorder (PTSD). Lance Cpl. Roel Ryan Briones, a Marine in Kilo Company, did not participate in the Haditha massacre. T. J. Terrazas was his best friend. Briones, who was 20 years old at the time, saw Terrazas after he was killed. "He had a giant hole in his chin. His eyes were rolled back up in his skull," Briones said of his buddy. "A lot of people were mad," Briones said. "Everyone had just a [terrible] feeling about what had happened to T.J."

After the massacre, Briones was ordered to take photographs of the victims and help carry their bodies out of their homes. He is still haunted by what he had to do that day. Briones picked up a young girl who was shot in the head. "I held her out like this," he said, extending his arms, "but her head was bobbing up and down and the insides fell on my legs. I used to be one of those Marines who said that post-traumatic stress is a bunch of bull," said Briones, who has gotten into serious trouble since he returned home. "But all this stuff that keeps going through my head is eating me up. I need immediate help."[29]

Regardless of how those who may ultimately be charged with crimes fare in court, a more significant question is whether Bush, Cheney, and Rumsfeld can be charged with war crimes on a theory of *command responsibility*. After the Haditha massacre, Hagee flew to Iraq to brief U.S. forces on the Geneva Conventions, the international laws of armed conflict, and the U.S. military's own rules of engagement. He reportedly told the troops they should use deadly force "only when justified, proportional and, most importantly, lawful."[30] Hagee's briefing creates a strong inference that our leaders had not adequately briefed our troops on how to behave in this war.

That inference, combined with the mounting evidence of other war crimes, has persuaded many observers that such incidents are a predictable consequence of the administration's actions. Retired Army General John Batiste said there was a "direct link" between the Haditha incident and the "bad judgment" of Donald Rumsfeld in 2003 and 2004. Batiste explained that Rumsfeld left troops "under-resourced [and] overcommitted," resulting in an "unbelievable" strain on U.S. forces.[31] Retired Air Force Col. Mike Turner, a former planner at the Joint Chiefs of Staff, also drew a line from the administration's chief officers to crimes on the ground in Iraq. "What we're seeing more of now, and these incidents will increase monthly, is the end result of fuzzy, imprecise national direction combined with situational ethics at the highest levels of this government."[32]

For his part, Congressman Murtha told ABC there was "no question" the U.S. military tried to "cover up" the Haditha incident, which Murtha called "worse than Abu Ghraib."[33] His high-level briefings indicated to him that the cover-up went "right up the chain of command."[34] Murtha said the decision to pay compensation to families of the victims is strong evidence that officers up the chain of command knew what had happened in Haditha. "That doesn't happen at the lowest level. That happens at the highest level before they make a decision to make payments to the families."[35]

Senator John Warner, R-Va., head of the Armed Services Committee, pledged to hold hearings on the Haditha killings at the conclusion of the military investigation. "I'll do exactly what we did with Abu Ghraib," he declared on ABC News.[36] Yet Congress has yet to hold our leaders to account for the torture at Abu Ghraib prison.

For all these reasons, Iraqis are dubious about the Bush administration's commitment to the rule of law. "America in the view of many Iraqis has no credibility. We do not believe what they say is correct," said Sheik Sattar al-Aasaaf, a tribal leader in Anbar province, which includes Haditha. "U.S. troops are very well-trained and when they shoot, it isn't random but due to an order to kill Iraqis. People say they are the killers."[37] The 24 Haditha victims are buried in a cemetery called Martyrs' Graveyard. Graffiti on the deserted house of one of the families reads, "Democracy assassinated the family that was here."[38]

ONE, TWO MANY HADITHAS

Allegations that U.S. troops have engaged in summary executions and willful killing in Iraq have also emerged from other Iraqi cities, including Qaim, Abu Ghraib, Taal Al Jal, Mukaradeeb, Mahmudiya, Hamdaniyah, Samarra, Salahuddin, and Ishaqi. There are similar accusations stemming from incidents in Afghanistan as well.

Some of these killings have occurred in prisons or at checkpoints. In an August 2003 e-mail, the office of the U.S. commander in Iraq instructed soldiers: "The gloves are coming off, gentlemen. . . . We want these individuals broken. Casualties are mounting." On September 10, the top commander authorized several new interrogation techniques, including one that Chief Warrant Officer Lewis Weishofer interpreted as permission to stuff Iraqi Maj. Gen. Abed Hamed Mowhoush into a sleeping bag, bind him with an electrical cord, straddle his chest, and intermittently cover his mouth. Mowhoush, who had been brutally beaten by CIA contractors, died in the sleeping bag on November 26, 2003, in Qaim. Weishofer was convicted of negligent homicide and negligent dereliction of duty. He received a letter of reprimand.[39]

Aidan Delgado, an Army reservist in the 320th Military Police Company, served in Iraq's Abu Ghraib prison from fall 2003 through March 2004. Delgado, who became a conscientious objector, reported that his fellow soldiers shot unarmed prisoners. During a demonstration by prisoners, some threw stones or pieces of wood at the guards. "One of my buddies got hit in the face," Delgado recalled. "He got a bloody nose. But he wasn't hurt. The guards asked permission to use lethal force. They got it." Delgado also said, "Killing noncombatants at checkpoints happened routinely, not only with the Third Infantry, but the First Marines." More than 50 prisoners were killed, Delgado observed, after being housed outside the prison, in the line of fire, with no protection.[40] The Fourth Geneva Convention forbids an occupying power from detaining protected persons in areas particularly exposed to the dangers of war unless the security of the population or imperative military reasons so demand.[41] The ICRC's report that 70% to 90% of those detained in Iraq were there by mistake was based on an estimate by coalition military intelligence officials.[42]

In early 2004, 22-year-old Edward Richmond, Jr., had been Iraq less than three weeks. U.S. Army Sgt. Jeffrey Waruch relayed orders to his squad to shoot any men fleeing the village of Taal Al Jal but to check with him if possible before firing. Richmond saw a cow herder in a nearby field and checked with Waruch. Their stories differ about whether Waruch gave Richmond permission to shoot. Richmond fired one shot into Muhamad Husain Kadir's head. Richmond, who suffers from PTSD, was convicted of voluntary manslaughter and sentenced to three years in prison, a demotion in rank, and a dishonorable discharge. Defense evidence that Waruch had shot three female civilians, one of whom died, was kept out of trial.[43]

U.S. troops killed more than 40 people during an attack on a wedding party in Mukaradeeb, a desert village near the Syrian border. A 30-year-old woman who survived the massacre told the *Guardian,* "We went out of the house and the American soldiers started to shoot us. They were shooting low on the ground and targeting us one by one." Haleema Shihab said that she ran with her two little boys. They were all shot. "I left them because they were dead. I fell into the mud and an American soldier came and kicked me. I pretended to be dead so he wouldn't kill me." Ma'athi Nawaf, another survivor, said, "I saw something that nobody ever saw in this world. There were children's bodies cut into pieces, women cut into pieces, men cut into pieces. . . . The Americans call these people foreign fighters. It is a lie."[44]

On March 12, 2006, a woman, her child, her husband, and her brother-in-law were killed in Mahmudiya. Fakhirya Taha Mmuhsen was raped before she was killed. "Never in my life could I have imagined such a gruesome sight," said Abu Firas Janabi, Fakhirya's cousin. "Kasim's corpse was in the corner of the room, and his head was smashed into pieces," and Abu could see that Fakhirya's arms had been broken. Steven Green, a former private with the 101st Airborne Division, was charged with rape and murder of the Mahmudiya family. He said, "I shot a guy who wouldn't stop when we were out at a traffic checkpoint and it was like nothing. Over here, killing people is like squashing an ant." Green cited the meaninglessness of the war: "See, this war is different from all the ones that our fathers and grandfathers fought. Those wars were for something. This war is for nothing." The Mahmudiya killings were originally reported by the military as being a result of "insurgent activity."[45] Still another cover-up.

A Navy corpsman and seven Marines who are members of Kilo Company were charged in the killing of an innocent Iraqi man on April 26, 2006. Hashim Ibrahim Awad al-Zobaie, a disabled 52-year-old man, was dragged from his home in Hamdaniyah and then shot to death. An AK-47 and a shovel were planted next to his body to make it look like he was burying an improvised explosive device (IED). Hashim's family reported that a group of U.S. servicemen offered them money to support the Marines' story of the killing.[46] One more cover-up.

The Monitoring Net of Human Rights in Iraq reported that on May 5, 2006, U.S. soldiers entered the home of an Iraqi family in Samarra and killed the father; mother; daughter, who was in the 6th grade; and son, who was suffering from mental and physical disabilities.[47] Four days later, four members of the 101st Airborne Division killed three detainees on an island near Samarra. They filed affidavits saying they had been given orders to "kill all military-age males."[48] The same day, three members of the 3rd Brigade Combat Team, 101st Airborne Division, killed three Iraqis in military custody in Salahuddin.[49]

On May 30, 2006, U.S. troops shot and killed two Iraqi women, one of whom was pregnant. They were on their way to the Samarra General Hospital, where Nabiha Nisaif Jassim was about to give birth. Although U.S. troops said their car failed to stop at a checkpoint after being warned to stop, the car was actually shot from behind by a U.S. sniper and there was no warning, according to an Iraqi human rights investigator who interviewed three eyewitnesses.[50]

A few days after the story of the Haditha massacre became public, U.S. forces killed 11 civilians after rounding them up in a room in a house in Ishaqi near Balad, handcuffing and shooting them. The victims ranged from a 75-year-old woman to a six-month-old child and included three-year-olds and five-year-olds and three other women as well.[51] A June 3 report by the U.S. military that found no wrongdoing by the U.S. soldiers drew a strong rebuke from Iraqi Prime Minister Nouri al-Maliki, who said the report clearing the soldiers was unfair.[52]

One of the first accounts of willful killing by U.S. forces after Bush's "war on terror" began arose at the U.S. military base in Bagram, Afghanistan. In December 2002, the bodies of two young Afghan men were found within days of each other; both had been hanged by their shackled wrists in their cells at the U.S. base in Bagram.[53]

Several incidents of U.S. attacks that indiscriminately killed civilians have been reported in Afghanistan. The worst occurred in July 2002, when Afghan officials said 48 civilians were killed and 117 were wounded during a bombing in Uruzgan province. Twenty-five members of an extended family attending a wedding celebration were among the dead. In April and May 2006, Afghan President Hamid Karzai complained twice in five weeks of civilian deaths from U.S.-led air strikes. One bombing killed at least 16 civilians, including some at a religious school. Another killed seven civilians in eastern Kunar province.[54]

In March 2003, the Green Berets tortured and killed two unarmed brothers in Wazi, Afghanistan. One surviving detainee said an interrogator ripped off one of his toenails; another alleged he had been subjected to water-boarding. The U.S. military initially reported that the death of Jamal Mohammed was caused by an illness. Naseer Mohammed's death was not reported to the office of the medical examiner, as required for deaths that do not result from natural causes. No charges have been filed in the case.[55]

One of Baghdad's senior medical officials told Robert Fisk at the Baghdad mortuary that "when the Americans bring bodies in, we are instructed that under no circumstances are we ever to do post-mortems."[56] Nouri al-Maliki charged in June 2006 that violence against civilians had become a "daily phenomenon" by many U.S. troops who, he said, "do not respect the Iraqi people." Reports of willful killing of civilians continue to emerge as Bush's illegal war claims increasing numbers of innocent people.

FOUR

-)))(-—)))(-—)))(-

THE GUANTANAMO GULAG

Travelers to Cuba and music lovers are familiar with the song "Guantanamera"— literally, the girl from Guantánamo. With lyrics by José Martí, the father of Cuban independence, "Guantanamera" is probably the most widely known Cuban song. But Guantánamo is even more famous now for its U.S. military prison. Whereas "Guantanamera" is a powerful expression of the beauty of Cuba, "Gitmo" has become a powerful symbol of human rights violations—so much so that Amnesty International has described it as "the gulag of our times."[1]

That description can be traced to January 2002, when the base received its first 20 prisoners in shackles. General Richard B. Myers, chairman of the Joint Chiefs of Staff, warned they were "very dangerous people who would gnaw hydraulic lines in the back of a C-17 to bring it down."[2] We now know that a large portion of the 750-plus men and boys held there posed no threat to the United States. In fact, only five percent were captured by the United States; most were picked up by the Northern Alliance, Pakistani intelligence officers, or tribal warlords, and many were sold for cash bounties.[3] "More than 250 prisoners have been released with no intimation that they did anything wrong," notes attorney Joseph Margulies. The chief interrogator at the base says 75 percent of the prisoners are no longer being questioned. Even the camp commander says that "many of the five hundred who remain could be released tomorrow at no risk to the United States."[4]

The Bush gang is holding these detainees in violation of U.S. and international law. Maintaining a prison camp at Guantánamo is itself illegal. So are imprisoning detainees (including children) indefinitely without charges and subjecting them to cruel, inhuman, and degrading treatment.[5] Despite the fact that the Supreme Court ruled that the Bush administration must comply with the Geneva Conventions and the Uniform Code of Military Justice, it continues to devise new strategies to deny the detainees their day in court.

AN ILLEGAL OCCUPATION

The Gitmo story starts in 1903, when the U.S. Army occupied Cuba after its war of independence against Spain. The Platt Amendment, which granted the United States the right to intervene in Cuba, was included in the Cuban Constitution as a prerequisite for the withdrawal of U.S. troops from the rest of Cuba. That provision provided the basis for the 1903 Agreement on Coaling and Naval Stations, which gave the United States the right to use Guantánamo Bay "exclusively as coaling or naval stations, and for no other purpose."[6]

In 1934, President Franklin D. Roosevelt signed a new treaty with Cuba that allows the United States to remain in Guantánamo Bay until the United States abandons it or until both Cuba and the United States agree to modify their arrangement. According to that treaty, "the stipulations of [the 1903] agreement with regard to the naval station of Guantánamo shall continue in effect."[7] That means Guantánamo Bay can be used only for coaling or naval stations. Additionally, article III of the 1934 treaty provides that the Republic of Cuba leases Guantánamo Bay to the United States "for coaling and naval stations." Nowhere in either treaty did Cuba give the United States the right to utilize Guantánamo Bay as a prison camp.

It is no accident that the Bush gang chose Guantánamo Bay as the site for its illegal prison camp. The administration has maintained that Guantánamo Bay is not a U.S. territory, and thus U.S. courts are not available to the prisoners there. But the United States, not Cuba, exercises exclusive jurisdiction over Guantánamo Bay. Amanda Williamson, a spokeswoman in the Red Cross Washington office, notes that prisoners there "have been placed in a legal vacuum, a legal black hole." The U.S. authorities, she claims, "have effectively placed them beyond the law."[8] Amnesty International has gone further, noting an obvious gap between U.S. rhetoric and practice: "Given the USA's criticism of the human rights record of Cuba, it is deeply ironic that it is violating fundamental rights on Cuban soil, and seeking to rely on the fact that it is on Cuban soil to keep the US courts from examining its conduct."[9]

"INDESCRIBABLE TORTURE"

Although the Torture Convention forbids the use of coercion under any circumstances to obtain information, prisoners released from Guantánamo have described assaults, prolonged shackling in uncomfortable positions, sexual abuse, and threats with dogs. Mustafa Ait Idr, an Algerian citizen who was living in Bosnia when he was sent to Guantánamo, charged that U.S. military guards jumped on his head, resulting in a stroke that paralyzed his face. They also broke several of his fingers and nearly drowned him in a toilet.[10] Mohammed Sagheer, a Pakistani cleric, claimed the wardens at Guantánamo used drugs "that made us senseless."[11] French citizen Mourad Benchellali, released from Guantánamo in July 2004, said, "I cannot describe in just a few lines the suffering and the torture; but the worst aspect of being at the camp was the despair, the feeling that whatever you say, it will never make a difference." Benchellali added, "There is unlimited cruelty in a system that seems to be unable to free the innocent and unable to punish the guilty."[12]

Australian lawyer Richard Bourke, who has represented many of the men incarcerated at Guantánamo, charged that prisoners have been subjected to "good old-fashioned torture, as people would have understood it in the Dark Ages." According to Bourke, "One of the detainees had described being taken out and tied to a post and having rubber bullets fired at them. They were being made to kneel cruciform in the sun until they collapsed."[13] Abdul Rahim Muslimdost, an Afghan who was released from Guantánamo in April 2005, said he suffered "indescribable torture" there.[14]

U.S. and international bodies have verified reports of torture and abuse. Physicians for Human Rights found that "the United States has been engaged in systematic psychological torture of Guantánamo detainees."[15] FBI agents saw female interrogators forcibly squeeze male prisoners' genitals and witnessed detainees stripped and shackled low to the floor for many hours.[16] In February 2006, the UN Human Rights Commission reported that the violent force-feeding of detainees by the U.S. military at its Guantánamo prison camp amounts to torture. After it visited the Guantánamo camp, the International Committee of the Red Cross strongly condemned the detention of the prisoners housed there, noting "a worrying deterioration in the psychological health of a large number of them."[17] A high-level military investigation concluded in 2005 that several prisoners were mistreated or humiliated.[18]

DUE PROCESS?

As more organizations reach similar conclusions about Bush's gulag, the Supreme Court has made it clear that the administration has crossed several legal lines. First, in *Rasul v. Bush*, the Court settled the jurisdictional question. The United States exercises "complete jurisdiction and control" over the Guantánamo Bay base, Justice Stevens wrote for the Court in June 2004. "Aliens held at the base, like American citizens, are entitled to invoke the federal courts' authority" under the habeas corpus statute to challenge their confinement.[19] In short, the Bush administration could no longer argue that anything goes at Gitmo.

On the same day, the Court strongly rebuked Bush's actions in another case, *Hamdi v. Rumsfeld*. Writing for the Court, Justice Sandra Day O'Connor noted, "We have long since made clear that a state of war is not a blank check for the President when it comes to rights of the Nation's citizens." The President could detain U.S. citizens engaged in armed combat against the United States, but these detainees must be given "a meaningful opportunity to contest the factual basis for that detention before a neutral decisionmaker."[20]

The ink was barely dry on these opinions when the Bush administration established the Combatant Status Review Tribunals (CSRT), ostensibly to comply with the *Rasul* ruling; but there is little evidence that CSRT provides a meaningful opportunity to challenge detention. The prisoner is not entitled to an attorney, only a "personal representative," and anything the detainee tells his personal representative can be used against him. After reviewing the cases of 393 detainees, one legal team found that in 96 percent of the cases, the government had not produced any witnesses or presented any documentary evidence to the detainee before the hearing. Detainees were allowed to see only summaries of the classified evidence offered against them, and that evidence was always presumed to be reliable and valid. Requests by detainees for witnesses were rarely granted. In addition, the personal representatives said nothing in 14 percent of the hearings and made no substantive comments 30 percent of the time. Some personal representatives even advocated for the government's position. In three cases, the detainee was found to be "no longer an enemy combatant," but the military continued to convene tribunals until they were found to be enemy combatants. These detainees were never told of the favorable ruling, and there was no indication they were informed or participated in the second or third hearings.[21]

Given this record, the study concluded that the government "is attempting to replace habeas corpus with this no hearing process." Attorney Joseph Margulies put it even more pointedly: "The C.S.R.T. is the first time in U.S. history in which the lawfulness of a person's detention is based on evidence secured by torture that's not shared with the prisoner, that he has the burden to rebut and without the assistance of counsel."[22] Amnesty International concurred: "The detainees' right to be presumed innocent, and treated as such, unless and until they are convicted in a fair trial, has been flouted by an administration which has repeatedly labeled them as 'terrorists.'"[23] There is little doubt that the CSRT violates the International Covenant on Civil and Political Rights, which prohibits arbitrary detention and guarantees a detainee the right to be informed of the reason for his detention, the right to prompt access to counsel of his choosing, the right to examine adverse witnesses and to call witnesses on his own behalf, and the right to the presumption of innocence.

Congress decided to respond to *Rasul* as well—not to ensure due process, but to prevent it. On December 30, 2005, it passed the Detainee Treatment Act (DTA),[24] which stripped U.S. federal courts of jurisdiction to hear habeas corpus petitions filed after the date of the DTA. The DTA granted the U.S. Court of Appeals for the District of Columbia Circuit exclusive jurisdiction to determine the validity of any final decision of the CSRT. That court could only review those decisions to make sure they were consistent with CSRT procedures, which are set forth by the Secretary of Defense, and the Constitution. Review of military commission decisions was not guaranteed unless the alien was sentenced to a term of imprisonment of 10 years or more in a capital case. Detainees could not challenge the conditions of their confinement if they filed after December 30, 2005.

After the passage of the DTA, the Supreme Court stepped in again. The Bush administration charged Salim Ahmed Hamdan, Osama bin Laden's driver, with one count of conspiracy "to commit . . . offenses triable by military commission," then tried to dismiss Hamdan's legal challenge to the military commission scheduled to hear his case. It also maintained that Common Article Three to the Geneva Conventions did not apply to al-Qaeda members; but in *Hamdan v. Rumsfeld*, the Court held that Congress did not intend to deny federal court jurisdiction to detainees like Hamdan, whose cases were already pending when the DTA was enacted. Moreover, it held that the Geneva Conventions did apply. Finally, the Court determined that Congress's Authorization for the Use of Military Force, passed the day after 9/11, did not expand Bush's authority to convene military commissions that did not comport with safeguards in the Uniform Code of Military Justice (UCMJ). All three cases—*Hamdi, Rasul*, and *Hamdan*—were widely regarded as setbacks for unbridled executive power.

Writing for the majority, Justice John Paul Stevens concluded that "the military commission convened to try Hamdan lacks power to proceed because its structure and procedures violate both the [Uniform Code of Military Justice] and the Geneva Conventions."[25] The civil liberties community hailed the ruling. Michael Ratner, president of the Center for Constitutional Rights, noted that the Court "upheld the rule of law in this country and determined that the executive has gone beyond the constitution and international law."[26]

THE MILITARY COMMISSIONS ACT OF 2006

The Bush gang was unrepentant. In September 2006, Bush announced that he was sending Khalid Sheikh Mohammed and 13 other alleged terrorists to Guantánamo to stand trial before military commissions. Bush said his administration had "largely completed our questioning of the men." Under interrogation, Mohammed had admitted to targeting office buildings in New York, Chicago, and Los Angeles; New York suspension bridges; the New York Stock Exchange and other financial targets; the Panama Canal; Big Ben in London; buildings in Israel; U.S. embassies in Australia, Japan, and Indonesia; Israeli embassies in Azerbaijan, India, Australia, and the Philippines; airliners throughout the world; and nuclear power facilities in the United States. Many doubted the veracity of his claims, which were likely obtained under torture.[27]

Bush also complained that "the Supreme Court's recent decision has impaired our ability to prosecute terrorists through military commissions and has put in question the future of the CIA program." This program included the infamous secret "black sites" in Eastern Europe where the CIA tortured detainees and hid them from the International Committee of the Red Cross in violation of the Geneva Conventions.[28]

The recent decision Bush had in mind was *Hamdan v. Rumsfeld,* in which the Court held that Bush's military commissions did not comply with the law. Bush called on Congress to define the "vague and undefined" terms in Common Article Three because U.S. military and intelligence personnel involved in capture and interrogation "could now be at risk of prosecution under the War Crimes Act." Bush called this risk of prosecution—not the alleged crimes that lay behind it—"unacceptable."

To immunize himself and his team from war crimes prosecutions, Bush rammed the Military Commissions Act of 2006 (MCA) through Congress, whose members were afraid to appear "soft on terror" before the 2006 elections. Unlike Geneva's Common Article Three, the MCA tolerates "outrages upon personal dignity, in particular humiliating and degrading treatment" and "the passing of sentences and the carrying out of executions without previous judgment pronounced by a regularly constituted court." Both are defined as grave breaches of Geneva's Common Article Three, which were punishable under the U.S. War Crimes Act. The MCA also grants retroactive amnesty to those who had committed an outrage upon personal dignity.

In some respects, the MCA offers a few small steps toward due process. It prevents presiding officers from excluding defendants from their own trials, provides a right to "examine and respond to" the evidence, and permits greater discovery of the evidence than was allowed under Bush's original military commissions. But the MCA still authorizes military commissions to admit hearsay and some evidence obtained by coercion or without a search warrant, and the government can still prevent the accused from seeing classified evidence. Most significantly, the MCA strips habeas corpus rights—the last chance at liberty for those unjustly held by the government—from all non-U.S. citizens, even though the Constitution permits Congress to suspend habeas corpus only "when in Cases of Rebellion or Invasion the public Safety may require it."[29]

The suspension of habeas corpus will certainly have profound effects on noncitizen detainees. Consider the case of Abu Bakker Qassim, an Uighur from China who was held at Guantánamo for four years. "I was locked up and mistreated for being in the wrong place at the wrong time during America's war in Afghanistan. Like hundreds of Guantánamo detainees, I was never a terrorist or a soldier. I was never even on a battlefield. Pakistani bounty hunters sold me and 17 other Uighurs to the United States military like animals for $5,000 a head. The Americans made a terrible mistake." How did Qassim obtain his release from Guantánamo? "It was only the country's centuries-old commitment to allowing habeas corpus challenges that put that mistake right—or began to. In May, on the eve of a court hearing in my case, the military relented, and I was sent to Albania along with four other Uighurs." Qassim added:

> Without my American lawyers and habeas corpus, my situation and that of the other Uighurs would still be a secret. I would be sitting in a metal cage today. Habeas corpus helped me to tell the world that Uighurs are not a threat to the United States or the West, but an ally. Habeas corpus cleared my name—and most important, it let my family know that I was still alive.[30]

Suspending habeas corpus is a stunning setback for civil liberties and due process. But equally startling is the fact that the MCA empowers the President to declare anyone, including U.S. citizens, living inside or outside the United States, "unlawful enemy combatants" and to imprison them indefinitely.[31] *Unlawful enemy combatant* is broadly defined as a person who has (1) engaged in hostilities or who has purposefully and materially supported hostilities against the United States or its allies or (2) been deemed an unlawful enemy combatant by a Combatant Status Review Tribunal or another competent tribunal established by the President or the Secretary of Defense. Anyone who donates money to a charity that turns up on Bush's list of "terrorist" organizations, or who speaks out against the government's policies could be declared an "unlawful enemy combatant."

Any alien unlawful enemy combatant subject to trial by military commission is precluded from invoking any of the protections of the Geneva Conventions as a source of rights at his trial. That means the accused cannot complain about being tortured or subjected to humiliating and degrading treatment during his trial in the military commission. In fact, the MCA prevents any person from citing Geneva protections in any habeas or civil action in any court of the United States, where one of the parties to the lawsuit is the United States or a current or former officer, employee, member of the Armed Forces, or other agent of the United States.

So how unconstitutional is the Military Commissions Act? Let us count the ways. The MCA violates the Suspension Clause of the Constitution by denying non-U.S. citizens any meaningful opportunity to challenge the legality of their detention. It violates the Geneva Conventions in two ways: by watering down protections of Common Article Three and by effectively granting retroactive amnesty to U.S. officials who have tortured detainees. It violates the Fifth Amendment by allowing evidence obtained by coercion and the Fourth Amendment by admitting evidence seized without a warrant. And it violates the Sixth Amendment by allowing hearsay and classified evidence, which the accused can only see in summary form.

The first case to go through a military commission reveals the hypocrisy of the Bush scheme. Australian citizen David Hicks, who was held for more than five years at Guantánamo, reported being sodomized, beaten, and subjected to forced injections by guards. He plead guilty and will serve nine months in an Australian prison. Like John Walker Lindh, Hicks had to agree to keep quiet about the torture. He was also forbidden from filing a lawsuit complaining of abuse or talking to the media for one year.[32] If Hicks was such a dangerous terrorist, why was he given a misdemeanor sentence? It was likely a political deal to defuse the issue in an upcoming Australian election. The irony is that to be released from Guantánamo, one must plead guilty. If the accused goes to trial in a military commission and is acquitted, he could be held forever as an unlawful enemy combatant.

GITMO AND ITS CRITICS

Guantánamo's very existence at this point harms America's international reputation. A January 2005 editorial in *Le Monde* concludes, "The simple truth is that America's leaders have constructed at Guantánamo Bay a legal monster." Moreover, it has created more enemies of the United States. Writing for the *New York Times*, Somini Sengupta maintains that Guantánamo Bay has been a setback in the war on terror insofar as it has "emerged as a symbol of American hypocrisy."[33] "Guantánamo provides rhetorical fodder for politicians seeking to bring down United States–allied rulers in their own countries," Sengupta notes, "and it offers a ready rallying point against American dominance, even in countries whose own police and military have been known for severe violations of human rights."[34]

The list of Guantánamo critics is a long one. Archbishop Desmond Tutu has called it a stain on the character of the United States.[35] Former UN Secretary General Kofi Annan said the United States must close the camp as soon as possible.[36] *The Economist* has called for the facility to be dismantled, described the treatment of the prisoners there as "unworthy of a nation which has cherished the rule of law since its very birth," and claimed that it "has alienated many other governments at a time when the effort to defeat terrorism requires more international co-operation in law enforcement than ever before." The National Lawyers Guild, Association of American Jurists, and Amnesty International have all called for closing the prison camp and releasing or charging prisoners with criminal offenses in accordance with international legal norms.

In May 2006, the Committee Against Torture, which evaluates compliance reports from all parties to the Torture Convention, concluded that the United States "should cease to detain any person at Guantánamo Bay and close this detention facility, permit access by the detainees to judicial process or release them as soon as possible, ensuring that they are not returned to any State where they could face a real risk of being tortured."[37] It also called on the United States to rescind any interrogation technique—including sexual humiliation, water-boarding, short shackling, and using dogs to induce fear—that constitutes torture or cruel, inhuman, or degrading treatment or punishment. Detaining persons indefinitely without charge, as the United States has done with most of the prisoners at Guantánamo, constitutes a per se violation of the Convention, the committee noted.[38]

Even President Bush has said he would like to close the Guantánamo prison because it damages America's image in the world.[39] Yet his administration is spending $30 million to construct permanent cells and planning a $125 million compound to hold the military commissions trials.[40] Michael Ratner has called the compound "another huge waste of taxpayer money . . . to carry out kangaroo trials that will never pass constitutional muster."[41]

THE HUMAN COST OF AN ILLEGAL POLICY

In addition to legal and political problems with Gitmo, there are the enormous human costs to be considered. Attorney Joseph

Margulies has been to death row in six states and watched his client be executed. But he notes, "I have never been to a more disturbing place than the military prison at Guantánamo Bay. It is a place of indescribable sadness, where the abstract enormity of 'forever' becomes concrete: this windowless cell; that metal cot; those steel shackles."[42]

We should not be surprised that such indescribable sadness produces suicides. In May 2006, two Guantánamo detainees tried to kill themselves by overdosing on antidepressant drugs. On June 10, three men killed themselves by hanging in their cells. The three men who committed suicide, Mani Shaman Turki al-Habardi al-Utaybi, Yasser Talal Abdulah Yahya al-Zahrani, and Ali Abdullah Ahmed, were being held indefinitely at Guantánamo. None had been charged with any crime. All had participated in hunger strikes and been force-fed. Utaybi had been cleared for transfer out of Guantánamo, but it was unclear whether he had been told he would be leaving.[43] Military officials characterized their deaths as a coordinated protest. The commander of the prison, Rear Adm. Harry B. Harris, Jr., called it "asymmetrical warfare."[44] Colleen Graffy, the deputy assistant secretary of state for public diplomacy, callously said taking their lives "certainly is a good PR move."[45]

Whereas the Bush administration sought to portray the three suicides as political acts of martyrdom, Shafiq Rasul, a former Guantánamo prisoner who himself participated in a hunger strike while there, disagreed. "Killing yourself is not something that is looked at lightly in Islam, but if you're told day after day by the Americans that you're never going to go home or you're put into isolation, these acts are committed simply out of desperation and loss of hope," he said. "This was not done as an act of martyrdom, warfare or anything else."[46]

In 2005, at least 131 Guantánamo inmates engaged in hunger strikes, and 89 had participated as of June 2006. Former military linguist Erik Saar reported that weekly suicide attempts occurred when he was stationed at Guantánamo. "The detainees felt that their situation was hopeless," he said.[47] "A stench of despair hangs over Guantánamo. Everyone is shutting down and quitting," said Mark Denbeaux, a lawyer for two of the prisoners there. His client, Mohammed Abdul Rahman, "is trying to kill himself" in a hunger strike. "He told us he would rather die than stay in Guantánamo," Denbeaux added.[48] According to Bill Goodman, the legal director of the Center for Constitutional Rights, "The total, intractable unwillingness of the Bush administration to provide any meaningful justice for these men is what is at the heart of these tragedies. This is an act of desperation because they have no way to prove their innocence. A system without justice is a system without hope," Goodman said.[49]

Meanwhile, the Bush gang has been conducting another secret program that defies our laws—its domestic surveillance operation. Continuing in its usurpation of unparalleled executive power, the Bush administration has set up a vast network of eavesdropping on the telephone calls and e-mail communications of Americans.

FIVE

-)K-)K-)K-

SPYING ON AMERICANS

We do not believe the Executive has, or should have, the in
herent constitutional authority to violate the law or infringe
the legal rights of Americans, whether it be a warrantless
break-in into the home or office of an American, warrantless
electronic surveillance, or a President's authorization to the
FBI to create a massive domestic security program based
upon secret oral directives.
— Final Report of the Church Committee, 1976[1]

On December 16, 2005, the *New York Times* unleashed a bombshell: George W. Bush had been secretly spying on Americans
without warrants since late 2001. The next day, Bush confirmed
that he had authorized the National Security Agency (NSA) "to
intercept the international communications of people with
known links to al Qaeda and related terrorist organizations." Two
days later, Alberto Gonzales verified that Bush empowered the
NSA to intercept the contents of communications where there is
a "reasonable basis to believe" that a party to the communication
is "a member of al Qaeda, affiliated with al Qaeda, or a member
of an organization affiliated with al Qaeda or working in support
of al Qaeda."[2] Nearly one month later, Bush announced that his
spying operation was called the "Terrorist Surveillance Program."[3]
    Bush's spying scheme has had little discernable impact on the

government's ability to prevent terrorist plots by al-Qaeda.[4] But wiretapping without probable cause or judicial oversight violates both the Foreign Intelligence Surveillance Act (FISA)[5] and the Fourth Amendment. Moreover, thousands of innocent people have been caught up in this web of surveillance, and there is reason to believe that the government is using it to spy on critics of administration policies.

COINTELPRO AND FISA

The Terrorist Surveillance Program harks back to the bad old days of FBI Director J. Edgar Hoover and his domestic spying programs. Beginning in the 1940s, the FBI began widespread illegal surveillance to threaten and silence Americans who had unorthodox political views. Especially during the McCarthy period of the 1950s, many Americans lost their jobs and were blacklisted or even jailed. Thousands of lives were shattered.

In 1956, the FBI launched COINTELPRO (counterintelligence program) to "expose, disrupt, misdirect, discredit and otherwise neutralize" political and activist groups. In the 1960s, the FBI targeted Dr. Martin Luther King, Jr., in a program called "Racial Matters." King's voter registration campaign in the South and his opposition to the Vietnam War raised the hackles of the FBI, which disingenuously claimed King's organization was being infiltrated by communists and expressed concern that King "represented a clear threat to the established order of the U.S."[6] The FBI went after King with a vengeance, tapping his telephones and securing very personal information, which it used to try to discredit him and even drive him to divorce and suicide.

Later, President Richard Nixon used national security wiretaps against his domestic opponents. A few months before the 1972 presidential election, five burglars with photographic and eavesdropping equipment broke into the Democratic National Committee headquarters at the Watergate complex in Washington, DC. Reporters Carl Bernstein and Bob Woodward of the *Washington Post* as well as congressional investigators and special prosecutors revealed Nixon's complicity in a massive conspiracy to cover up the politically motivated break-in. Nixon's overreaching during the Watergate scandal led to his impeachment and resignation.

In response to the abuses by Nixon and the FBI, a Senate select committee chaired by Senator Frank Church began to investigate domestic intelligence activities in 1973. The Church Committee concluded in its 1977 report: "Since the 1930's, intelligence agencies frequently wiretapped and bugged American citizens without the benefit of judicial warrant in the absence of any genuine threat to national security." It also noted that "vast amounts of information—unrelated to any legitimate government interest—about the personal and political lives of American citizens" might be used "for partisan political and other improper ends by senior administration officials."[7]

With broad bipartisan support, Congress enacted the Foreign Intelligence Surveillance Act (FISA) in 1978 to regulate electronic surveillance while at the same time protecting national security. That law established the Foreign Intelligence Surveillance Court whose judges, appointed by the Chief Justice of the U.S. Supreme Court, meet in secret to consider applications by the government for wiretap orders. In those meetings, the government must convince a judge there is probable cause to believe that the target of the surveillance is a foreign power or the agent of a foreign power.

FISA does not apply to wiretaps of foreign nationals abroad. Its restrictions are triggered only when the surveillance targets a U.S. citizen or permanent resident or when the surveillance is obtained from a wiretap physically located within the United States. Also, FISA specifically covers warrantless wiretaps during wartime, limiting them to the first 15 days after war is declared. Congress has never suspended the application of FISA in times of war or other armed conflict, nor has it altered this 15-day limit on emergency wiretaps without court order.

There is only one other exception to the rule against warrantless electronic surveillance in FISA. For that exception to apply, the Attorney General must certify under oath that the communication to be monitored will be exclusively between foreign powers, and that there is no substantial likelihood that a U.S. person will be overheard. The law also specifies that FISA and provisions of Title III of the federal criminal code are the "*exclusive* means by which electronic surveillance . . . may be conducted."[8] However, FISA allows the Attorney General to wiretap in emergency situations without a prior judicial order, provided he or she applies for one within 72 hours after initiating the surveillance. The record indicates that FISA has not unduly constrained the executive branch's ability to engage in foreign intelligence surveillance. Between 1979 and 2003, the FISA court denied only three of the government's 16,450 applications for a warrant.[9]

AN END RUN AROUND FISA

President Bush has frequently reassured the country that our constitutional guarantees are safe. For example, in April 2004 he said,

> Now, by the way, any time you hear the United States government talking about wiretap, it requires—a wiretap requires a court order. Nothing has changed, by the way. When we're talking about chasing down terrorists, we're talking about getting a court order before we do so . . . constitutional guarantees are in place when it comes to doing what is necessary to protect our homeland, because we value the Constitution.[10]

The President was lying. In fact, the NSA had been spying on U.S. citizens without warrants for two and half years. Despite FISA's mandates and its streamlined procedure for allowing lawful surveillance, Bush intentionally sidelined the Foreign Intelligence Surveillance Court.

In late 2001, Bush signed a secret executive order establishing his Terrorist Surveillance Program. It authorized the NSA to eavesdrop on telephone and computer communications of Americans in the United States if the NSA—not a judge—decides there is "reasonable suspicion" to believe that one party is a member or agent of al-Qaeda or an affiliated terrorist organization, provided one party to the conversation is overseas. Despite the requirement that one end of the conversation take place on foreign soil, Bush's spying program has captured purely domestic communications. The government is listening to as many as 500 people at any given time, and the NSA has eavesdropped on thousands of private conversations since the program began.[11]

CIA Director Michael Hayden, who was director of the NSA from March 1999 through May 2005, said the decision about whose communications to spy on is made by operational people at the agency and "must be signed off by a shift supervisor." This is an inadequate substitute for a judge. Hayden said the program was "targeted and focused" and did not amount to a "driftnet" over the United States. He compared the techniques the NSA employed in the program to those used in deciding whether to drop a 500-pound bomb on a terrorist target.[12]

In a February 2003 report on FISA implementation failures, the Senate Judiciary Committee uncovered several problems, including "a misunderstanding of the rules governing the application procedure, varying interpretations of the law among key participants, and a breakdown of communication among all those involved in the FISA application process." Most disturbing to the committee was "the lack of accountability that has permeated the entire application procedure."

Judges on the Foreign Intelligence Surveillance Court were alarmed by Bush's end run. The *Washington Post* reported:

> Several FISA judges said they . . . remain puzzled by Bush's assertion that the court was not "agile" or "nimble" enough to help catch terrorists. The court had routinely approved emergency wiretaps 72 hours after they had begun, as FISA allows, and the court's actions in the days after the Sept. 11 attacks suggested that its judges were hardly unsympathetic to the needs of their nation at war.[13]

FISA's chief judge Colleen Kollar-Kotelly worried that information obtained by the NSA program was being improperly used as the basis for FISA wiretap requests.[14] Judge Royce Lamberth, who preceded Kollar-Kotelly as chief judge of the FISA court, was also concerned "that the president's program, if ever made public and challenged in court, ran a significant risk of being declared unconstitutional."[15] Once the program was publicly disclosed, FISA judge James Robertson was so troubled about its legality that he resigned in protest.[16]

When five former FISA judges testified before the Senate Judiciary Committee in March 2006, they urged Congress to give the Foreign Intelligence Surveillance Court a formal role in overseeing the NSA surveillance program. Judge Harold A. Baker said the President was bound by the law "like everyone else." He added, "If a law like the Foreign Intelligence Surveillance Act is duly enacted by Congress and considered constitutional, the president ignores it at the president's peril."[17] Indeed, Bush is the first President to defy FISA since it was enacted in 1978.[18]

On January 5, 2006, the nonpartisan Congressional Research Service issued a 44-page analysis that concluded the NSA program was unlawful. The report said it "appears unlikely that a court would hold that Congress has expressly or impliedly authorized the NSA electronic surveillance operations."[19] "What we have here," an editorial in the *New York Times* observed, "is a clandestine surveillance program of enormous size, which is being operated by members of the administration who are subject to no limit or scrutiny beyond what they deem to impose on one another. If the White House had gotten its way, the program would have run secretly until the war on terror ended— that is, forever."[20]

. . . AND AROUND THE FOURTH AMENDMENT

When the Founding Fathers put the Fourth Amendment into the Constitution, they were reacting against a police state in which the king's men broke into homes without warrants based on probable cause. The electronic update came in 1967, when the Supreme Court held in *Katz v. United States* that government wiretapping must be supported by a search warrant based on probable cause and issued by a judge.

Although the Court noted that its holding did not extend to cases involving national security, in a 1972 decision it rejected President Nixon's request to conduct warrantless electronic surveillance of domestic organizations without foreign ties, even for reasons of national security. The Court stated, "These Fourth Amendment freedoms cannot properly be guaranteed if domestic security surveillances may be conducted solely within the discretion of the Executive Branch." Moreover, the Court observed,

> Fourth Amendment protections become the more necessary when the targets of official surveillance may be those suspected of unorthodoxy in their political beliefs. The danger to political dissent is acute where the Government attempts to act under so vague a concept as the power to protect "domestic security."[21]

The decision did not examine the scope of the President's surveillance power regarding the activities of foreign powers. To fill this gap, Congress enacted FISA.

When questioned about the Fourth Amendment during his CIA director confirmation hearing, General Michael Hayden defended the NSA's warrantless surveillance program, assuring the Senate committee that he had consulted with relatives in law school for legal advice. Thus advised, Hayden reversed the Supreme Court's century-long Fourth Amendment jurisprudence. He told the senators that only reasonableness, not a warrant, is necessary to intercept private communications. Although Hayden said the NSA uses a probable cause standard, the Supreme Court has consistently declared that a *judge* must determine whether probable cause exists. The Senate confirmed Michael Hayden as director of the CIA, but both the American Bar Association and the National Lawyers Guild declared that Bush's warrantless surveillance program is illegal.[22]

GONZALES DEFENDS BUSH'S SNOOPING

After the *New York Times* revealed the existence of the NSA spying program, Attorney General Alberto Gonzales was called to testify before the Senate Judiciary Committee. He said the government still uses FISA in some cases but did not respond when Senator Arlen Specter asked him why he didn't seek FISA court approval for the broad NSA program. Gonzales refused to say whether he tells the FISA court that the administration uses information gathered through the NSA program to support a warrant request. He also declined to tell Specter whether the FISA court is refusing to issue warrants because it is not satisfied with the NSA program.[23]

Although FISA allows the government to seek a court order up to three days after it conducts electronic surveillance, Gonzales told the committee that the FISA procedure was "burdensome." Both the Department of Justice and the NSA have batteries of lawyers, but Gonzales said we "can't afford to pose layers of lawyers" in the process. Yet even former Secretary of State Colin Powell acknowledged that it would not have been "that hard" for the administration to obtain warrants to comply with the requirements of FISA.[24]

Gonzales also insisted that the FISA law allows for electronic surveillance without following FISA procedures, where such surveillance is "authorized by statute." Gonzales maintained that Congress's Authorization for the Use of Military Force (AUMF), passed shortly after the 9/11 attacks, was a statute that authorized surveillance outside of FISA. The AUMF permits the President to use "necessary and appropriate force" against "nations, organizations, or persons" that "planned, authorized, committed, or aided" the 9/11 attacks or that "harbored such persons."[25] Tom Daschle, who was Senate majority leader when Congress passed the AUMF, wrote in the *Washington Post*, "I helped negotiate that law with the White House counsel's office over two harried days. I can state categorically that the subject of wiretaps of American citizens never came up." Daschle was "confident that the 98 senators who voted in favor of authorization of force against al-Qaeda did not believe that they were also voting for warrantless domestic surveillance." In fact, Daschle wrote,

> Literally minutes before the Senate cast its vote, the administration sought to add the words "in the United States and" after "appropriate force" in the agreed-upon text. This last-minute change would have given the president broad authority to exercise expansive power not just overseas—where we all understood he wanted authority to act—but right here in the United States, potentially against American citizens.

The additional language was omitted from the final bill.[26]

Indeed, Congress made 25 separate amendments to FISA in the USA Patriot Act in October 2001, the month *after* Congress passed the AUMF. For example, it extended the period during which the government could request a FISA Court warrant from 24 hours after it began surveillance to 72 hours. When Gonzales was asked why the administration didn't approach Congress to amend FISA again if it needed more flexibility to fight terrorism, he said amending FISA would interfere with the NSA spying program.

Gonzales also claimed that the President's powers as commander in chief allow him to authorize warrantless wiretaps. But the President may not decide that a law such as FISA is somehow exempt from his constitutional duty to "take care that the laws be faithfully executed."[27] And, as Justice Robert Jackson wrote in the seminal case of *Youngstown Sheet & Tube Co. v. Sawyer*, the President's power is "at its lowest ebb" when he acts in defiance of "the expressed or implied will of Congress."[28] Nowhere is Congress's intent expressed more clearly than in FISA, which Congress specified to be the exclusive scheme for electronic surveillance to gather foreign intelligence.

At the end of the Congressional hearing, Gonzales let slip the real reason Bush set up a program to evade FISA. Gonzales said that if the government had to apply for a FISA warrant, it "can't begin surveillance based on a *whim* of someone at NSA." He would not tell the senators whether Bush has authorized other secret programs, and he refused to say whether the government could wiretap purely domestic calls without a warrant, search the first-class mail of American citizens, or examine people's medical records. But in a January 19, 2006, white paper that Gonzales submitted to Congress to justify the NSA surveillance program, Justice Department lawyers (including John Yoo, who helped draft the notorious torture memo) made the astounding claim that Bush also had the inherent authority to order warrantless physical searches.[29]

Former Colorado Senator Gary Hart, a member of the Church Committee in the 1970s, said, "What we're experiencing now, in my judgment, is a repeat of the Nixon years. Then it was justified by civil unrest and the Vietnam War. Now it's terrorism and the Iraq war."[30] Bush has already gone far beyond what the Constitution authorizes, and FISA makes it a crime, punishable by up to five years in jail, for the executive to conduct a wiretap without statutory authorization.

MINING PERSONAL DATA

The Terrorist Surveillance Program is not the only secret surveillance operation Bush has authorized. In another bombshell, *USA Today* revealed in May 2006 that Verizon Communications, AT&T, and BellSouth had provided the NSA with telephone and Internet communications flowing into and out of the United States.[31] Through this program, the NSA has collected vast personal information about millions of people that has nothing to do with national security. Verizon and BellSouth, both facing lawsuits for invasion of privacy, issued qualified denials, and AT&T has refused comment.[32]

Our government is reportedly not listening to the content of the communications but rather tracking them in a huge database. But as the *New York Times* reported the same month, "One senior government official who was granted anonymity to speak publicly about the classified program confirmed that the NSA had access to records of most telephone calls in the U.S."[33] Sources advised Seymour Hersh that the NSA was monitoring domestic calls on a "real-time" basis, and a security consultant working with a major telecommunications carrier told Hersh, "What the companies are doing is worse than turning over records. They're providing total access to all the data."[34] Interestingly, Bush issued an executive order on May 5 that allows

Director of Intelligence John Negroponte to authorize a company to conceal activities related to "national security."[35] This means we cannot trust the denials by Verizon and BellSouth.

Like Bush's warrantless eavesdropping on phone calls, the NSA's massive data collection is illegal. In particular, telephone records that show what numbers have called a specific telephone are captured by a "trap and trace" device. A "pen register" reveals what number a specific telephone has called. The Pen Register and Trap and Trace Statute prohibits the installation of any pen register or trap and trace device without first obtaining a court order either under FISA or Title III, the criminal wiretap law. The data mining program also likely violates the 1986 Stored Communications Act.[36]

If the NSA spying program and the data mining operation weren't enough, the Bush gang initiated another secret plan to collect our most personal information, called the Terrorist Finance Tracking Program. Without seeking court-approved warrants or subpoenas, counterterrorism officials have accessed financial records from a huge international database and examined the banking transactions of thousands of Americans in the United States. L. Richard Fischer, a leading expert on banking privacy, said that the use of broad subpoenas to demand large volumes of financial records for analysis would apparently constitute an end run around bank-privacy laws that usually require the government to demonstrate the records of a particular person or group are relevant to an investigation.[37]

SPYING LEADS TO DEAD ENDS

When Gonzales testified before the Senate committee, he continually waved the 9/11 flag in defense of Bush's secret spying program. Bush called the operation a "vital tool" against terrorism, and Cheney claimed it has saved "thousands of lives."[38] Yet the *Washington Post* reported that nearly all of the thousands of Americans' calls that have been intercepted have revealed nothing pertinent to terrorism.[39] According to a January 17, 2006, report in the *New York Times,*

> More than a dozen current and former law enforcement and counterterrorism officials, including some in the small circle who knew of the secret program and how it played out at the FBI, said the torrent of tips led them to few potential terrorist inside the country they did not know of from other sources and diverted agents from counterterrorism work they viewed as more productive.

A former senior prosecutor reported that intelligence officials who turned over tips "would always say that we had information whose source we can't share, but it indicates that this person has been communicating with a suspected Qadea operative." The prosecutor said, "I would always wonder, what does 'suspected' mean?" He added, "The information was so thin and the connections were so remote, that they never led to anything, and I never heard any follow-up."[40]

After the *Times* article was published, Hayden claimed that if the NSA program had been operating before the September 11 attacks, "it is my professional judgment that we would have detected some of the 9/11 al Qaeda operatives in the United States." Neither he nor Cheney, who had made a statement similar to Hayden's, mentioned the 9/11 Commission's finding that the NSA, CIA, and FBI had important information about two of the highjackers in January 2000 but failed to capitalize on it. Hayden also neglected to point out that the NSA had intercepted warning of the attacks on September 10 but didn't have it translated until September 12.[41]

Why is the Bush administration loath to obtain warrants to authorize wiretaps? "The most logical reason for not getting a warrant is that the president's intelligence acolytes, who behave as though they graduated from the Laurel and Hardy school of data mining, have not been able to demonstrate that the people being spied upon are connected to Al Qaeda or any other terror organization," Bob Herbert wrote in the *New York Times*.[42] In other words, even the super-secret FISA court may be refusing to give Bush what he wants because he is overreaching.

Bruce Fein, who served as associate deputy attorney general in the Reagan administration, predicted that Bush's theory of expanded executive power could be used to authorize internment camps for groups of American citizens the President deems suspicious.[43] Senator Richard Durbin (D-Ill.) said, "Our concern is that what this president is asking for will allow this administration to comb through thousands of ordinary Americans' e-mails and phone calls."[44]

BIG BROTHER IS WATCHING — AND LISTENING

Since September 11, 2001, the Bush gang has methodically chipped away at our civil liberties. The month after the 9/11 attacks, Attorney General John Ashcroft, inspired by John Yoo, rammed the USA Patriot Act through a shell-shocked Congress with almost no congressional comment. Besides amending FISA and establishing other provisions to facilitate surveillance and detention, the Patriot Act created a crime of domestic terrorism aimed at political activists who protest government policies and set forth an ideological test for entry into the United States. The FBI rates the Animal Liberation Front and Earth Liberation Front as the number one domestic terrorist threats, calling eco-sabotage the government's top domestic terrorism priority. In 2004, the government launched "Operation Backfire" to target environmental activists, conducting large-scale roundups of activists, levying unprecedented penalties for property crimes, and using threats of severe sanctions to leverage fear of conviction and force individuals to turn state's evidence.[45]

Shortly after Congress enacted the Patriot Act, the Pentagon developed a tracking system called Total Information Awareness (TIA), which would have been capable of searching public and private databases and combining the information to find patterns and associations of 300 million Americans.[46] Congress eliminated the funding for the controversial TIA in September 2003; but it has been replaced by several other programs, including the Pentagon's "Threat and Local Observation Notice" (TALON) Program, that have collected information on innocent U.S. citizens at churches, libraries, and college campuses, including peace activists at the Quaker Meeting House in Lake Worth, Florida. A senior Pentagon official estimated that the number of reports with names of U.S. persons could be in the thousands.[47]

Another result of Watergate and COINTELPRO was Attorney General Edward Levi's establishment of guidelines to reign in the FBI.[48] On May 30, 2002, John Ashcroft and FBI Director Robert Mueller unveiled sweeping new surveillance powers for the FBI, removing a number of the safeguards Levi had put in place 26 years before.[49] To cover its own incompetence in failing to analyze properly the data it already had before September 11, the FBI was given wide latitude to spy more effectively on law-abiding citizens.

Under what New York Times columnist William Safire characterized as "the new Ashcroft-Mueller diktat,"[50] the FBI could conduct investigations for up to a year without the necessity of showing any suspicion of criminal activity. The G-men and G-women could create dossiers on anyone they like, tracking the Internet sites we visit, trips we take, our political and charitable contributions, magazine subscriptions, book purchases, and meetings we attend. Anyone perceived as critical of the government was fair game for an FBI "fishing expedition."

In an October 2003 memo, the FBI urged law enforcement agencies to monitor the Internet because "protestors often use the Internet to recruit, raise funds and coordinate their activities prior to demonstrations," according to a report in the *New York Times*.[51] The Justice Department's Office of Legal Counsel (OLC), the same group that wrote the memos advising Bush how to get away with torturing prisoners, blessed the 2003 FBI memo. The OLC said that interrogating and gathering evidence on potential political protestors raised no First Amendment concerns. Any "chilling" effect, it noted, would be "quite minimal" and was far outweighed by the overriding public interest in maintaining "order."[52]

The FBI's drive to collect intelligence related to protests has resulted in the harassment of people engaging in protected First Amendment activity. For example, in February 2004, the government sought to use a federal grand jury in Iowa to harass and intimidate antiwar protestors. A Polk County deputy sheriff who worked with the FBI's Joint Terrorism Task Force (JTTF) subpoenaed Drake University and four peace activists to produce records about a National Lawyers Guild conference that featured nonviolence training for people planning to demonstrate the next day at an antiwar rally at the Iowa National Guard headquarters. Twelve protestors were arrested at the peaceful rally, titled "Stop the Occupation! Bring the Iowa Guard Home!" The subpoenas requested the agenda and purpose of the meeting, the identities of attendees and Guild officers, and observations of campus security. Those served with subpoenas included the leader of the Catholic Peace Ministry, the former coordinator of the Iowa Peace Network, a member of the Catholic Worker House, and an antiwar activist who had visited Iraq in 2002.

According to the U.S. Attorney's office, the sole intent of the subpoenas was to gather information about a solitary demonstrator who scaled a fence on federal property on a different day from the antiwar conference/training. Why, then, did the government issue five subpoenas calling for information about peaceful activists and the National Lawyers Guild? Iowa Sen. Tom Harkin complained, "I don't like the smell of it . . . It reminds me too much of Vietnam when war protestors were rounded up, when grand juries were convened to investigate people who were protesting the war."[53] The subpoenas constituted a flagrant attack on constitutionally protected speech and association. In response to the Guild's opposition and widespread outrage throughout the country, they were withdrawn one week later.

In 2005, NBC News obtained a secret 400-page Defense Department document that included a Department of Defense (DoD) database with nearly four dozen antiwar meetings or protests, some of which took place far from any military facility or recruitment center.[54] A Freedom of Information Act request revealed that counterterrorism agents at the FBI have conducted extensive surveillance of such groups as the Vegan Community Project, the People for the Ethical Treatment of Animals, and a Catholic Workers group the FBI accuses of having a "semi-communist ideology."[55] Red-baiting is once again alive and well in America.

The JTTF in the FBI's Pittsburgh office conducted a secret investigation of the Thomas Merton Center from November 2002 through March 2005. The center is an interfaith organization whose members believe in nonviolent struggle for peace and justice. A November 29, 2002, FBI report identified the center as "a left-wing organization advocating, among many political causes, pacifism." The report noted that one person handing out antiwar leaflets "appeared to be of Middle Eastern descent." Tim Vining, the center's former executive director, said, "All we want to do is exercise our First Amendment rights . . . Is handing out fliers now considered a terrorist activity?"[56]

In a March 2006 report by the Justice Department Inspector General, the FBI reported more than 100 possible violations of the Patriot Act during the preceding two years. These included incidents where agents tapped the wrong telephone, intercepted the wrong e-mails, or continued listening to conversations after the warrant had expired. One year later, the Inspector General revealed that the FBI illegally used the Patriot Act to collect data on Americans and then lied to Congress about it.[57]

At the same time, internal NSA documents show that the agency used local law enforcement agencies, including the Baltimore Police Department, to monitor members of a city antiwar organization who were preparing a protest outside Fort Meade. The target of the secret surveillance was the Baltimore Pledge of Resistance, a group affiliated with the American Friends Service Committee, which engaged in nonviolent civil disobedience.[58] A file on the Pentagon's surveillance activities from November 2004 to May 2005 lists spying on antiwar protestors in 20 different states and the District of Columbia.[59] This surveillance is reminiscent of the infamous COINTELPRO, which the FBI used to pursue those who challenged the government's policies.

According to John Dean, counsel to President Nixon, "With NSA listening to some five-hundred telephone calls at any given time and apparently potentially capturing millions of others, mountains of digital information are accumulating. There is no oversight of the NSA program. And under the Patriot Act, the information NSA is gathering can be shared with other law enforcement agencies."[60]

WATCH WHAT YOU SAY, WATCH WHAT YOU DO

Justice Louis Brandeis, in his 1928 dissent in *Olmstead v. United States*, cautioned, "The greatest dangers to liberty lurk in insidious encroachment by men of zeal, well meaning but without understanding." Seventy-three years later, former White House spokesman Ari Fleischer, speaking for an overly zealous President, cautioned Americans "they need to watch what they say, watch what they do."[61]

In a November 2006 speech at the Air Force Academy, Alberto Gonzales ominously warned that those who say Bush's surveillance program stifles freedom constitute "a grave threat to the liberty and security of the American people."[62] Likewise, documents obtained by the American Civil Liberties Union under a Freedom of Information Act request show that military officials labeled antiwar rallies and anti–military recruitment as "potential terrorist activity." When Bush's secret surveillance program was revealed, he called the leak a "shameful act" that is "helping the enemy."[63] Dick Cheney concurred: "Some in the press, in particular the *New York Times*, have made the job of defending against further terrorist attacks more difficult by insisting on publishing detailed information about vital national security programs."[64]

But Cheney also revealed a historical motive behind Bush's assertion of executive power when he observed, "Watergate and a lot of the things around Watergate and Vietnam, both during the 1970s, served, I think, to erode the authority I think the president needs to be effective, constitutional powers unimpaired."[65] No one expressed that view of presidential authority better than former President Richard Nixon. In a 1977 interview with David Frost, Nixon explained his interpretation of executive privilege: "When the President does it, that means it's not illegal."[66] A generation later, Nixon's counsel, John Dean, wrote, "In some two hundred and seventeen years of the American presidency, there has been only one President who provides a precedent for Bush's stunning, in-your-face, conduct: Richard Nixon. Like Bush," Dean observed, "Nixon claimed he was acting to protect the nation's security. Like Bush, Nixon broke the law, authorizing, among other things, illegal wiretaps."[67] Former President Carter, who signed FISA into law in 1978, took a similar line: "Under the Bush administration, there's been a disgraceful and illegal decision—we're not going to let the judges or the Congress or anyone else know that we're spying on the American people," Carter said. "And no one knows how many innocent Americans have had their privacy violated under this secret act."[68]

Bush's warrantless wiretaps have resurrected a longstanding American debate about the proper balance between liberty and security. When I asked Associate Justice Ruth Bader Ginsburg if the balance would be slanted away from liberty in the wake of September 11, she replied, "The nation has been tested before . . . and we haven't come through very well," referring to the internment of Japanese-Americans during World War II and President Abraham Lincoln's suspension of civil liberties during the Civil War. She added, "One can hope we've learned from those past experiences, but the returns aren't in."

In light of those experiences, many Americans share Benjamin Franklin's view: "They who would give up an essential liberty for temporary security, deserve neither liberty nor security." Certainly that view was reinforced by executive overreaching in the 1970s and earlier, which gave rise to safeguards like FISA. Yet Church's warnings have lost none of their relevance. In 1975, he said of the NSA's powers of surveillance, "That capability at any time could be turned around on the American people, and no American would have any privacy left, such is the capability to monitor everything: telephone conversations, telegrams, it doesn't matter. There would be no place to hide." And he provided an ominous warning: "I don't want to see this country ever go across the bridge. I know the capacity that is there to make tyranny total in America, and we must see to it that this agency [NSA] and all agencies that possess this technology operate within the law and under proper supervision, so that we never cross over that abyss. That is the abyss from which there is no return."[69] Church could not have foreseen the development of e-mail and cell phones, but he understood that new technologies would only intensify the problem. Now more than ever, we are One Nation Under Surveillance.

SIX

-)))(—)))(—)))(-

REFUSING TO
EXECUTE THE LAW

Our Founding Fathers created three separate, co-equal branches of government to check and balance each other so that no one branch would become all powerful. Indeed, James Madison wrote in the *Federalist Papers*, "The preservation of liberty requires that the three great departments of power should be separate and distinct." Madison warned, "The accumulation of all powers, legislative, executive, and judiciary, in the same hands . . . may justly be pronounced the very definition of tyranny."[1] This was not a hollow fear. The American colonists had suffered mightily at the hands of the tyrant King George III. Thus they charged in the Declaration of Independence that the King has "refused his Assent to Laws, the most wholesome and necessary for the public good."

Two hundred and twenty years later, we have another King George. Since he became President in 2001, George W. Bush has increasingly sought to accumulate all governing powers in the same hands—his. Contrary to the Constitution's command that the President "shall take Care that the Laws be faithfully executed,"[2] Bush has repeatedly violated some of them and refused to enforce others, including those governing nuclear proliferation.

But he has also asserted unparalleled executive power by putting his stamp of supremacy on more than one thousand provisions of law enacted by Congress. The Constitution grants Congress the power to make laws, and after both houses pass a bill, the President has two options: he can either sign it or veto it. In his first six years in office, Bush vetoed only one bill—the stem cell research law. Yet he has quietly attached "signing statements" to 1,132 laws passed by Congress. The language of these statements is obscure, but they declare his intention to violate the law. Rather than veto laws he disagrees with, Bush has used his signing statements as a line-item veto, indicating which parts of each law he intends to enforce—despite the fact that the Supreme Court has ruled that the line-item veto is unconstitutional.[3]

George W. Bush hasn't only defied Congress; he has also usurped the power of the courts, which have exclusive jurisdiction to interpret the laws. The Supreme Court said, "It is, emphatically, the province and duty of the judicial department to say what the law is."[4] When judges review statutes for constitutional infirmity, they frequently look to legislative history by referring to the *Congressional Record*. Presidential signing statements do not constitute legislative history, and the courts do not use them for statutory interpretation. But Bush's signing statements frequently graft his own interpretation onto the law, reserving the right to refuse to follow those parts he deems unconstitutional.

Although the Constitution nowhere authorizes signing statements, presidents dating back to James Monroe have employed them; but none before George W. Bush has used them so extensively to shift the balance of power to the President. That shift has some vocal advocates. When he was deputy assistant attorney general in the Reagan administration, Supreme Court Justice Samuel Alito argued for enhancing the role of presidential signing statements. He advised the Office of Legal Counsel, "Our primary objective is to ensure that Presidential signing statements assume their rightful place in the interpretation of legislation." Although he admitted that Congress would resent the use of signing statements that allow the President to "get in the last word on questions of interpretation," Alito advocated "the issuance of interpretive signing statements" to "increase the power of the Executive to shape the law."[5]

Faced with a Congress controlled by Democrats, Ronald Reagan began to use signing statements to put his political imprimatur on congressional legislation. Reagan's attorney general, Edwin Meese, sought to make presidential signing statements part of the legislative history by arranging to have them published in the *U.S. Code Congressional and Administrative News*. Meese said, "To make sure that the President's own understanding of what's in a bill is the same . . . or is given consideration at the time of statutory construction later on by a court, we have now arranged with West Publishing Company that the presidential statement on the signing of a bill will accompany the legislative history from Congress so that all can be available to the court for future construction of what that statute really means."[6]

Courts have declined to use presidential signing statements as authoritative legislative history. Nonetheless, Bush continues to employ them to rewrite myriad laws. By December 25, 2006, Bush had issued a total of 147 signing statements, which included 1,132 distinct challenges to provisions of law. "The administration does a shuck and jive with the figures, suggesting that they have issued fewer signing statements than previous presidents, which is true. But the devil is in the details—he has blown the lid off the number of challenges—1,132," said Miami University political science professor Christopher Kelley, an expert on presidential power. "By the end of his first term,"

Kelley added, "he had issued more challenges than all previous presidents combined."[7]

THE UNITARY EXECUTIVE

Many of Bush's signing statements say that he will follow the statutory provision consistent with the powers of "the unitary executive." A seemingly innocuous phrase, this term actually represents a radical, ultra–right wing interpretation of the powers of the presidency. Championed by the conservative Federalist Society, the unitary executive doctrine gathers all power in the hands of the President and insulates him from any oversight by the congressional or judicial branches. In a November 2000 speech to the Federalist Society, then-Judge Samuel Alito said the Constitution "makes the president the head of the executive branch, but it does more than that. The president has not just some executive powers, but the executive power—the whole thing."[8] These "unitarians" claim that all federal agencies, even those constitutionally created by Congress, are beholden to the Chief Executive, that is, the President. This means that Bush could disband agencies like the Federal Communications Commission, the Food and Drug Administration, and the Federal Reserve Board, if they weren't to his liking. Indeed, Bush signed an executive order stating that each federal agency must have a regulatory policy office run by a political appointee. Consumer advocates were concerned that this directive was aimed at weakening the Environmental Protection Agency and the Occupational Safety and Health Administration. The unitary executive dogma represents audacious presidential overreaching into the constitutional province of the other two branches of government.

This doctrine took shape within the Bush administration shortly after 9/11. On September 25, 2001, former Deputy Assistant Attorney General John Yoo used the words *unitary ex-*

ecutive in a legal memo he wrote for the White House: "The centralization of authority in the president alone is particularly crucial in matters of national defense, war, and foreign policy, where a *unitary executive* can evaluate threats, consider policy choices, and mobilize national resources with a speed and energy that is far superior to any other branch."[9] Six weeks later, Bush began using that phrase in his signing statements.[10] As of December 22, 2006, Bush had used the words *unitary executive* 145 times in his signing statements and executive orders.[11] Yoo, one of the chief architects of Bush's doctrine of unfettered executive power, wrote memoranda advising Bush that because he was commander in chief, he could make war anytime he thought there was a threat, and he didn't have to comply with the Geneva Conventions. In a December 1, 2005, debate with Notre Dame professor Doug Cassel, Yoo argued there is no law that could prevent the President from ordering that a young child of a suspect in custody be tortured, even by crushing the child's testicles.[12] In John Yoo's world, the President is the law.

Similar language has already cropped up in Supreme Court opinions. In his lone dissent in *Hamdi v. Rumsfeld*, Justice Clarence Thomas cited "the structural advantages of a unitary Executive." He disagreed with the Court that due process demands an American citizen held in the United States as an enemy combatant be given a meaningful opportunity to contest the factual basis for that detention before a neutral decision maker. Thomas wrote, "Congress, to be sure, has a substantial and essential role in both foreign affairs and national security. But it is crucial to recognize that *judicial* interference in these domains destroys the purpose of vesting primary responsibility in a unitary Executive."[13]

In 1926, Justice Louis Brandeis explained the constitutional role of the separation of powers. He wrote, "The doctrine of the separation of powers was adopted by the convention of 1787 not to promote efficiency but to preclude the exercise of arbitrary power. The purpose was not to avoid friction, but, by means of the inevitable friction incident to the distribution of the governmental powers among three departments, to save the people from autocracy."[14] Eighty years later, noted conservative Grover Norquist, describing the *unitary executive* theory, echoed Brandeis' sentiment. Norquist said, "You don't have a constitution; you have a king."[15]

SIGNING AWAY CHECKS AND BALANCES

Let's examine some of King George W. Bush's signing statements. He issued his most notorious one after he signed the Detainee Treatment Act in December 2005, which prohibited the United States from subjecting prisoners to cruel, inhuman, or degrading treatment or punishment. It also upheld federal court access for Guantánamo detainees whose habeas corpus petitions were already pending.[16] The Bush gang resisted the measure, which was proposed as an amendment to an appropriations bill for the Iraq and Afghanistan wars. Bush finally signed the bill with great fanfare. He then quietly attached a signing statement declaring that his administration would interpret the new law "in a manner consistent with the constitutional authority of the President to supervise the unitary executive branch and as Commander in Chief and consistent with the constitutional limitations on the judicial power."[17] These words are tantamount to saying Bush will follow the law when he wants and refuse to do so when he doesn't.

The Supreme Court didn't buy it. In *Hamdan v. Rumsfeld*, the high court made no mention of Bush's signing statement when it rejected the President's contention that the Detainee Treatment Act did not apply to pending habeas corpus peti-

REFUSING TO EXECUTE THE LAW

tions of Guantánamo detainees. In his dissent, Justice Antonin
Scalia chided the majority for ignoring Bush's signing statement,
but Justice John Paul Stevens, writing for the Court's majority,
categorically declared that "the Executive is bound to comply
with the Rule of Law."[18]

Bush made good on his vow to violate the Detainee Treatment Act. His gang continues to subject prisoners to cruel, inhuman, and degrading treatment, notwithstanding the dictates
of the Detainee Treatment Act that Congress passed. Although
Bush denies that U.S. forces are torturing and mistreating prisoners, an American who was mistakenly detained by U.S. authorities reported being subjected to what amounts to cruel,
inhuman, and degrading treatment for three months in mid-
2006. Donald Vance was a Navy veteran who worked in Iraq as
a security contractor. While he was there, Vance became an in-
formant for the FBI, blowing the whistle on possible illegal arms
trading. While Vance was held at Camp Cropper in Baghdad,
U.S. military personnel subjected him to 24-hour florescent
lights in his cell, constant blaring of heavy metal or country
music, and forced standing in his cell. Five months after Vance
was released, he still suffers from nightmares, depression, shame,
and paranoia.[19]

Another signing statement that garnered intense opposition
when it became public followed the renewal of the USA Patriot
Act. Bush and the Congress had fought a pitched battle over the
legislation. Following the revelation of Bush's secret executive
order creating his warrantless domestic spying program, the
Senate refused to renew the Patriot Act, which was set to expire
on December 31, 2005. After granting an extension, the Senate
eventually agreed to the bill three months later.[20] The new law
contained several provisions requiring congressional oversight
so Congress could ensure that the Justice Department was not

illegally violating the privacy of Americans. When Bush signed the bill in a White House ceremony, he called it "a piece of legislation that's vital to win the war on terror and to protect the American people."[21] Then he quietly issued a signing statement citing "the President's constitutional authority to supervise the unitary executive branch and to withhold information the disclosure of which could impair foreign relations, national security, the deliberative processes of the Executive, or the performance of the Executive's constitutional duties."[22] In other words, Bush reserved the right to refuse to turn over the reports Congress mandated when it renewed the Patriot Act.

Bush's signing statement propelled House Intelligence Committee Ranking Member Jane Harman and House Judiciary Committee Ranking Member John Conyers, Jr., to send a letter of protest to Attorney General Alberto Gonzales. Citing Bush's claim of "authority to ignore reporting requirements to Congress," the lawmakers wrote, "The signing statement, and many of the 107 similar statements the President has issued on other legislation, have the effect of corrupting the legislative process. Indeed, during consideration of this matter, many Members who supported the final law did so based upon the guarantee of additional reporting and oversight. This Administration cannot, after the fact, unilaterally repeal provisions of the law implementing such oversight."[23]

In response to the publication of reports of Bush's secret domestic spying program, Congress passed a law mandating the Defense Department to provide Congress with "a report providing a comprehensive inventory of Department of Defense Intelligence and intelligence-related programs and projects."[24] Bush responded by issuing a signing statement directing the Defense Department essentially to ignore the statute.[25]

It is well established that Congress may impose reporting requirements on Executive Branch officials.[26] Yet Bush has issued other signing statements saying he can decline to provide Congress with reports from the Defense Secretary detailing the conduct of military operations for Operation Enduring Freedom in Afghanistan, plans for ballistic missile defense systems, and discussions with Russia on nonproliferation agreements. He says he can make the CIA refuse to report to Congress on intelligence activity and decline to require the Inspector General (IG) of the Justice Department and the Attorney General to document oversight of the FBI. Bush's signing statements also would prevent the National Board for Education Services from chronicling the progress in improving the nation's educational system.

There was a public outcry when the *Washington Post* revealed that Bush had signed an executive order establishing secret "black sites" where prisoners were illegally secreted from the International Committee of the Red Cross and many subjected to torture. Yet after Congress passed legislation requiring the President to tell Congress before diverting funds from authorized programs to "special access programs," such as the "black sites," Bush maintained he had the right to refuse to so notify Congress.

When he signed the bill in which Congress authorized him to use military force against Iraq, Bush wrote, "While I appreciate receiving that support, my request for it did not, and my signing this resolution does not, constitute any change in the long-standing positions of the executive branch on either the President's constitutional authority to use force to deter, prevent, or respond to aggression or other threats to U.S. interests or on the constitutionality of the War Powers Resolution."[27] The Constitution gives only Congress the power to declare war; the President has no authority to mount a war of aggression as Bush did when he invaded Iraq.[28]

In 1978, Congress passed the Office of Inspector General
Act, which requires the IG in every U.S. government agency to
investigate every complaint that agency receives and report its
findings to Congress.[29] As a result, IGs provide independent
oversight to keep our government honest. There is much corruption to investigate in Iraq. In an August 2005 interview,
Former Army Reserve Brigadier General Janis Karpinski told me
that she "saw corruption like I've never seen before—millions of
dollars just being pocketed by contractors. Everything was on a
cash basis at that time," she said. "You take a request down—
literally, you take a request to the Finance Office. If the Pay
Officer recognized your face and you were asking for $450,000
to pay a contractor for work, they would pay you in cash:
$450,000. Out of control."[30]

Congress enacted a law in November 2003 requiring that
the IG in Iraq tell Congress whenever officials refuse to cooperate with its investigations.[31] Bush declared in his signing statement that the IG need not issue such notification to Congress.[32]
One year later, Congress passed a law that created a Special
Inspector General for Iraq Reconstruction to succeed the Coalition Provisional Authority and required the IG to conduct investigations and report to Congress.[33] In his signing statement,
Bush wrote that this Special IG "shall refrain" from investigating
intelligence or national security matters or any crime the Pentagon decides it wants to investigate.[34] So much for accountability
for our tax dollars in Iraq.

The Bush gang frequently touts its support for our troops,
some of whom are on their fifth tour of duty in Iraq and
Afghanistan. But Bush issued a signing statement scoffing at the
limits Congress has placed on the number of days a member of
the Armed Forces may be deployed. Bush has also reserved the
right to disobey congressional mandates that the Defense Secre-

tary report to Congress about whether the prohibition against requiring injured troops to pay for their hospital meals is being enforced and about the effectiveness of detection and diagnosis of Post Traumatic Stress Disorder. He has likewise signed away his obligation to have his Defense Secretary institute studies about brain injuries suffered by our troops and mental health benefits for members of the Armed Forces.

In other signing statements, Bush has indicated he will not follow laws that:

- Ban the use of U.S. combat troops against Colombian rebels
- Forbid the use in military intelligence of evidence collected in violation of the Fourth Amendment
- Mandate new regulations for military prisons in which military lawyers could advise commanders on the legality of certain treatment even if Justice Department lawyers disagree
- Require the retraining of prison guards in humane treatment under the Geneva Conventions
- Mandate background checks for civilian contractors in Iraq
- Prohibit the firing or punishment of employee whistleblowers at the Department of Energy and the Nuclear Regulatory Commission
- Require expanded recruitment of minorities for Foreign Service and Civil Service jobs
- Direct the Department of Homeland Security to tell Congress when it is unable to deploy explosive detection systems at airports.

Contrast Bush's signing statements with the one President Jimmy Carter issued when he signed the Foreign Intelligence Surveillance Act in 1978. Carter wrote:

The bill requires, for the first time, a prior judicial warrant for *all* electronic surveillance for foreign intelligence or counterintelligence purposes in the United States in which communications of U.S. persons might be intercepted. It clarifies the Executive's authority to gather foreign intelligence by electronic surveillance in the United States. It will remove any doubt about the legality of those surveillances which are conducted to protect our country against espionage and international terrorism. It will assure FBI field agents and others involved in intelligence collection that their acts are authorized by statute and, if a U.S. person's communications are concerned, by a court order. And it will protect the privacy of the American people. In short, the act helps to solidify the relationship of trust between the American people and their Government. It provides a basis for the trust of the American people in the fact that the activities of their intelligence agencies are both effective and lawful. It provides enough secrecy to ensure that intelligence relating to national security can be securely required, while permitting review by the courts and Congress to safeguard the rights of Americans and others.[35]

Whereas Bush purports to rewrite the laws Congress has passed, Carter sought to underscore the importance of following them.

The nonpartisan Congressional Research Service, in its September 2006 report, determined that Bush's use of signing statements is emblematic of his "comprehensive strategy to strengthen and expand executive power." Arlen Specter, the Republican senator from Pennsylvania and former chairman of the Senate Judiciary Committee, pointed out that Bush is trying to do an end run around the veto process. Specter said, "Under the Constitution if the president doesn't like a bill he vetoes it. You don't cherry-pick the legislation."[36]

In one of his last signing statements of 2006, Bush declared that he considered as only "advisory" Congress's directive prohibiting transfers of certain nuclear material to India.[37] In doing so, he highlighted his refusal to execute the law governing one of the most critical issues of our time—nuclear proliferation.

COURTING NUCLEAR DISASTER

Throughout his presidency, Bush has thumbed his nose at our legal obligations under the 1970 Nuclear Non-Proliferation Treaty (NPT). When the United States ratified this treaty, it became part of the supreme law of the land under the Supremacy Clause of the Constitution. The treaty commits the countries that possess nuclear weapons (Britain, China, France, Russia, and the United States) to negotiate their elimination. To gain the agreement of the non–nuclear-weapon parties to the treaty's extension in 1995, the United States made promises in connection with a UN Security Council resolution calling for what are known as *negative security assurances*, in which the U.S. promised not to use nuclear weapons against non–nuclear-weapon parties unless they attack the United States while in alliance with another nuclear-weapon country.

The International Court of Justice (World Court) issued an advisory opinion on the legality of the threat or use of nuclear weapons in 1996. The World Court said that under humanitarian law, countries must "never use weapons that are incapable of distinguishing between civilian and military targets." It held that the threat or use of nuclear weapons was generally contrary to international law. Although the divided Court was unable to reach a definitive conclusion regarding threat or use in extreme circumstances of self-defense where the survival of a nation was at stake, the overall thrust of the decision was toward categorical illegality. It strongly implied that the doctrine of deterrence is illegal. The Court said the radioactive effects of nuclear explosions cannot be contained in space and time.[38] Thus, the use of nuclear weapons can never conform to the requirements of the law.

In 2002, Bush's Defense Department presented its Nuclear Posture Review (NPR) to Congress, which actually expands the range of circumstances in which the United States could use nuclear weapons. This document explicitly allows the option of using nuclear weapons against non-nuclear nations. It permits preemptive attacks against biological and chemical weapons capabilities and in response to "surprising military developments." It provides for the development of nuclear warheads, including earth penetrators. Alarmingly, classified portions of the NPR obtained by the *Los Angeles Times* and the *New York Times* call for contingency planning for the use of nuclear weapons against Russia, China, North Korea, Iraq, Iran, Syria, and Libya.[39]

When the NPR was introduced in 2002, the *New York Times* said, "Where the Pentagon review goes very wrong is in lowering the threshold for using nuclear weapons and in undermining the effectiveness of the Nuclear Nonproliferation Treaty. . . . Nuclear weapons are not just another part of the military arsenal. They are different, and lowering the threshold for their use is reckless folly."[40] Yet according to the Lawyers' Committee on Nuclear Policy, today the United States stands "ready to rapidly launch 2,000 strategic warheads with land- and submarine-based missiles. Each warhead would inflict vast heat, blast and radiation seven to 30 times that of the Hiroshima bomb."[41]

The Pentagon's March 2005 "Doctrine for Joint Nuclear Operations" would allow the United States to use nuclear weapons to counter potentially overwhelming conventional adversaries, to secure a rapid end of a war on U.S. terms, or simply "to ensure success of US and multinational operations"—a shockingly broad permission. This also violates the NPT.

Under the NPT, countries that don't have nuclear weapons

agreed not to acquire them in exchange for the promise from nuclear states to disarm progressively. Disarmament and nonproliferation are two sides of the same coin or two contractual promises exchanged. Thus, when the Bush administration unilaterally decides not to disarm, but instead to develop and even contemplate using new nukes, it stands in flagrant violation of the NPT. Bush cannot "choose" nonproliferation over disarmament.

The Bush administration's nuclear policy is not just illegal and hypocritical. It's downright dangerous. When North Korea and Iran—two members of Bush's "axis of evil"—see the third member invaded and occupied by the Bush gang, coupled with Bush's aggressive development of nuclear weapons, it is hardly surprising that they would develop their own nukes.

THE PRESIDENT CANNOT BE A LAWMAKER

Bush has frequently rationalized his overreaching across the lines separating the three branches of government by professing the need to protect the American people against terrorism. We have seen this in Bush's claims of authority to hold prisoners indefinitely with no access to courts and to listen in on our conversations without a warrant. In his signing statements, Bush asserts the right to violate the will of Congress because he is commander in chief and the "unitary executive."

This is by no means a new issue. During the Korean War, President Harry Truman claimed he had "inherent power" under his authority as commander in chief to seize America's steel mills for the war effort, proclaiming "the existence of a national emergency." In a landmark ruling in 1952, *Youngstown Sheet & Tube Co. v. Sawyer*, the Supreme Court disagreed, saying the seizure did not stem from a congressional policy prescribed by Congress but rather from an executive policy prescribed by the President. Significantly, the Court held that Truman's seizure violated the constitutional doctrine of separation of powers despite what the President claimed was an emergency that threatened the ability of the United States to defend itself. The Court held that "In the framework of our Constitution, the President's power to see that the laws are faithfully executed refutes the idea that he is to be a lawmaker. The Constitution limits his functions in the lawmaking process to the recommending of laws he thinks wise and the vetoing of laws he thinks bad."[42]

Justice Robert Jackson's famous concurrence in *Youngstown* is widely cited as a formula for gauging the powers of the President in relationship to Congress. Jackson wrote: "(1) When the President acts pursuant to an express or implied authorization of Congress, his authority is at its maximum, for it includes all that he possesses in his own right plus all that Congress can delegate. . . . (2) When the President acts in absence of either a congressional grant or denial of authority, he can only rely upon his own independent powers, but there is a zone of twilight in which he and Congress may have concurrent authority, or in which its distribution is uncertain. . . . (3) When the President takes measures incompatible with the expressed or implied will of Congress, his power is at its lowest ebb, for then he can rely only upon his own constitutional powers minus any constitutional powers of Congress over the matter."[43]

When Bush sets up his secret spying program in violation of Foreign Intelligence Surveillance Act (FISA), when he establishes military commissions that violate Congress's Uniform Code of Military Justice, when he defies the Nuclear Non-Proliferation Treaty, and when Bush attaches signing statements to congressional bills indicating his intention to defy the will of Congress, he falls squarely into Jackson's third category.

The Task Force on Presidential Signing Statements and the Separation of Powers Doctrine of the American Bar Association

(ABA) decried Bush's use of signing statements as "contrary to the rule of law and our constitutional system of separation of powers." The ABA's blue-ribbon task force found Bush has used his signing statements to "claim the authority or state the intention to disregard or decline to enforce" laws adopted by Congress. In its report, the task force urged the President to communicate his concerns about legislation to Congress prior to passage and to use his veto power if he thinks all or part of a bill is unconstitutional. It urged Congress to enact legislation requiring the President to submit to Congress promptly all signing statements he issues as well as his rationale for their issuance and to pass legislation allowing the President, Congress, or other entities or individuals to seek judicial review of any presidential claim to disregard or decline to enforce all or part of any law he has signed.

"The President's constitutional duty is to enforce the laws he has signed into being unless and until they are held unconstitutional by the Supreme Court or a subordinate tribunal," the task force concluded. "The Constitution is not what the President says it is."[44] ABA president Michael S. Greco cautioned, "We will be close to a constitutional crisis if this issue, the president's use of signing statements, is left unchecked."[45]

Bruce Fein, deputy attorney general in the Reagan administration and one of the members of the ABA's task force, testified at the Senate Judiciary Committee's June 2006 hearing on presidential signing statements. Fein warned of the disastrous consequences of Bush's use of signing statements. "Suppose Congress were to enact a law forbidding the President to employ military force in Iran aiming to destroy its nuclear facilities," Fein told the senators. "President Bush might sign the law but in a signing statement declare that he would treat it as advisory to preserve his Commander in Chief prerogatives. The ability of

Congress to participate in shaping the foreign relations and national security of the United States would be crippled, and the express congressional authority to enact laws to regulate the constitutional powers of the President in Article I, section 8, clause 18 would be a dead letter."[46]

New York University law professor David Golove, an expert on executive power, said Bush has cast a cloud over "the whole idea that there is a rule of law." A president like Bush, who ignores the rulings of the Supreme Court, coupled with a Congress that is unwilling to stand up to him can simply make the Constitution "disappear," Golove noted.[47] Professor Edward Herman of the University of Pennsylvania issued a similar warning. "The brazenness of Bush's use of [signing statements] is remarkable," Herman said. "But even more remarkable is the fact that this de facto further nullification of congressional authority fails to elicit sustained criticism and outrage. It is part of a step-by-step abrogation of constitutional government, and it is swallowed by the flag-wavers and normalized. We are in deep trouble," Herman added.[48]

In a 2006 speech marking the birthday of Martin Luther King, Jr., former Vice President Al Gore warned, "An Executive who arrogates to himself the power to ignore the legitimate legislative directives of the Congress or to act free of the check of the judiciary becomes the central threat that the Founders sought to nullify in the Constitution—an all-powerful Executive too reminiscent of the King from whom they had broken free."[49] Eight days before Bush penned his infamous intent to disobey the Detainee Treatment Act, Senator Edward M. Kennedy wrote in the *Boston Globe*, "The president is not above the law; he is not King George."[50]

The Constitution is unequivocal. It is George W. Bush's job to enforce, not to rewrite, the laws Congress has passed. If we allow our President to become a King, we will find ourselves in the same predicament that spawned the American Revolution. As the Founding Fathers wrote in the Declaration of Independence, "When a long train of abuses and usurpations, pursuing invariably the same Object evinces a design to reduce them under absolute Despotism, it is their right, it is their duty, to throw off such Government, and to provide new Guards for their future security."

CONCLUSION

In January 2007, George W. Bush responded to the American people's overwhelming opposition to the Iraq war by deciding to "sacrifice" more than 20,000 additional U.S. troops to that conflict. Bush had cowed Congress into capitulating to his wars on Iraq and on the Constitution, but lawmakers in both parties finally stood up to him, albeit timidly. As this book goes to press, President Bush is furiously resisting all efforts to bring the troops home for good.

Would the new Democratic-controlled Congress stop Bush's attack on civil liberties? More than 200 years ago, the Alien and Sedition Acts of 1798 backfired. They unified the Republican Party, Thomas Jefferson was elected president, and the Republicans secured a majority in the House of Representatives. The Sedition Act, now universally considered unconstitutional, expired on March 3, 1801, the last day of John Adams' term. Jefferson's first presidential act was to pardon all who had been convicted under that nefarious law. Today Congress has the power to prevent the Bush gang from establishing a police state.

As this book goes to press, many feared Bush was planning to attack Iran. He rattled the sabers and opted for gunboat diplomacy by pledging to "seek out and destroy" Iranian networks "providing advanced weaponry and training to our enemies" in Iraq. But he has produced no hard evidence that Iran is supplying forces in Iraq with such weapons or manufacturing their own nuclear weapons. Nevertheless, Bush sent U.S. warships and Patriot missile batteries to the Persian Gulf and moved U.S. attack aircraft to Turkey and other countries on Iran's borders. U.S. forces stormed the Iranian consulate in northern Iraq, capturing six Iranian nationals, and Bush announced he would go after any Iranians he considered a threat. Like the war on Iraq, an invasion of Iran would violate both the U.S. Constitution and the UN Charter. Moreover, it would spell certain disaster both in the Middle East and throughout the world.

THE DUTY TO DISOBEY

The war in Iraq has garnered strong opposition, even resistance, within the military. In June 2006, U.S. Army First Lt. Ehren Watada became the first commissioned officer to refuse publicly his orders to deploy to Iraq. Watada said, "The war in Iraq is in fact illegal. It is my obligation and my duty to refuse any orders to participate in this war." He stated, "An order to take part in an illegal war is unlawful in itself. So my obligation is not to follow the order to go to Iraq." Citing "deception and manipulation . . . and willful misconduct by the highest levels of my chain of command," Watada declared there is "no greater betrayal to the American people" than the Iraq war. The "turning point" for him came when he "saw the pain and suffering of so many soldiers and their families, and innocent Iraqis." He added, "I best serve my soldiers by speaking out against unlawful orders of the highest levels of my chain of command, and making sure our leaders are held accountable." Watada felt he "had the obligation to step up and do whatever it takes," even if that means facing court-martial and imprisonment.[1] Charged with missing movement and conduct unbecoming an officer, Lt. Ehren Watada was facing six years in the brig as we went to press.

Several soldiers and sailors, including Pablo Paredes, Camilo Mejía, Aidan Delgado, Jeremy Hinzman, Augustín Aguayo, Mark Wilkerson, Katherine Jashinski, Kyle Snyder, Ricky Clousing, Darrell Anderson, Ivan Brobeck, Suzanne Swift, and Kevin Benderman, are modern-day war resisters. At his court-martial, Paredes maintained that transporting Marines to fight in an illegal war and possibly commit war crimes would make him complicit in those crimes. He told the judge, "I believe as a member of the armed forces, beyond having a duty to my chain of command and my President, I have a higher duty to my conscience and to the supreme law of the land. Both of these higher duties dictate that I must not participate in any way, hands-on or indirect, in the current aggression that has been unleashed on Iraq." I testified at Paredes' court-martial to corroborate his claim that the war was illegal and if he deployed with his ship, he could be complicit in the commission of war crimes. The Navy judge gave Paredes no time in jail.

Both the Nuremberg Principles and the Uniform Code of Military Justice establish the duty to obey lawful orders, but they also recognize a duty to disobey unlawful orders. The Nazi defendants at Nuremberg argued unsuccessfully that they were just obeying superior orders when they committed atrocities during the Holocaust. Lt. William Calley, who was tried for his role in the 1968 My Lai Massacre during the Vietnam War, also said he was just following orders. His defense was rejected.

The war in Iraq is illegal. Soldiers who fight in Iraq are placed in the position of committing war crimes, such as torture, inhuman treatment, and summary execution of prisoners. Because the war is unlawful, orders to deploy to Iraq are unlawful orders.

In January 2006, an Appeal for Redress signed by nearly 1,000 uniformed military personnel was delivered to Congress. It called for the United States to withdraw from Iraq. Several dozen officers, including colonels, were signatories to the Appeal. The GI Rights Hotline estimated that 1,000 or more troops and reservists go AWOL (absent without leave) each month and between 200 and 300 have fled to Canada. The National Lawyers Guild's Military Law Task Force receives about 3,000 calls a month from disaffected soldiers and sailors.

Contemporary military resistance has its roots in the GI movement that played a critical role in ending the Vietnam War more than thirty years ago. The revelation of massive war crimes during the My Lai Massacre turned GIs against that war. They realized that U.S. government policy created My Lai. Unlike the Vietnam era, however, the United States no longer conscripts its youth into the war machine. The absence of a universal draft has left college students on the sidelines, complacent about the military actions in Iraq and Afghanistan. Soldiers and sailors voluntarily enlist now, so what right do they have to complain? The "poverty draft" that sweeps youth into the military is a new phenomenon that makes warfare painless for upper- and middle-class America. Military recruiters target poor kids from small rural communities and inner cities who face shrinking job markets. Desperate to meet enlistment quotas, recruiters frequently lie to prospective recruits.

Cindy Sheehan, whose son Casey died shortly after he arrived in Iraq, galvanized the antiwar movement and resistance within the military when she set up camp down the road from Bush's ranch in Crawford, Texas, and demanded an audience with Bush. Sheehan said, "I was told my son was killed in the war on terror. He was killed by George Bush's war of terror on the world."

INVESTIGATE THE BUSH GANG

Before the Democrats took control of Congress in 2007, efforts to investigate prewar intelligence distortion and manipulation and the legality of the National Security Agency's spying program were stopped in their tracks by the Justice Department and the GOP-led legislature.

Congress should immediately convene a nonpartisan independent inquiry conducted by a commission such as the 9/11 panel, followed by full congressional hearings like the Senate Watergate hearings. The commission should have access to all records, including presidential documents, prepared during the run-up to the war and regarding rules of engagement and the treatment of prisoners in U.S. custody, and the domestic surveillance program. It should also question high government officials, up to and including George W. Bush.

If the inquiry determines that the President, Vice President, Secretary of Defense, or any senior government officials knew or should have known of the torture and abuse, a special prosecutor should be appointed to determine whether there is criminal liability under the War Crimes Act, the Torture Statute, and other applicable criminal statutes. The prosecutor must be fully independent, with no ties to the Bush administration or its opponents.

U.S. Department of Justice regulations call for the appointment of an outside special counsel when (1) a criminal investigation of a person or matter is warranted, (2) the investigation or prosecution of that person or matter by a U.S. Attorney's Office or litigating Division of the Department of Justice would present a conflict of interest for the Department, and (3) under the circumstances it would be in the public interest to appoint an outside Special Counsel to assume responsibility for the matter.

When these three conditions are satisfied, the Attorney General must select a special counsel from outside the government.[2]

A criminal investigation is warranted. Alberto Gonzales, who is implicated in the commission of criminal offenses,[3] cannot be counted on to prosecute the guilty because he has a conflict of interest. The public interest demands that justice be done for the commission of these egregious crimes, which have violated basic American values, damaged America's reputation, and exposed us to increased danger.

Mindful that a Democratic-controlled Congress would mean embarrassing, perhaps incriminating, investigations of wrongdoing, the Bush gang fired several U.S. attorneys and replaced them with Bush loyalists. A little-noticed change slipped into the Patriot Act had stripped federal judges of their power to appoint U.S. attorneys and handed it to the Attorney General. The Bush gang had planned ahead.

PROSECUTE THE BUSH GANG IN THE UNITED STATES

From September 2002 through March 2003, right up until the invasion of Iraq, Bush and his senior administration officials insisted they had not decided whether to attack Iraq. The Downing Street Minutes confirmed agreements had been made between the Bush and Blair governments in the spring and summer of 2002 to go to war in Iraq. The Bush gang's marketing campaign to sell the war to the American people and its efforts to use the United Nations as a pretext to go to war in late 2002 and early 2003 corroborate their conspiracy. George W. Bush, Dick Cheney, Donald Rumsfeld, Condoleezza Rice, and Colin Powell should be prosecuted for conspiracy to defraud the United States for their fraudulent misrepresentations about the need to go to war with Iraq.[4]

By ratifying the Torture Convention and the Geneva Conventions, the United States undertook an obligation to punish those who have committed torture and war crimes. The torture and inhuman treatment of prisoners in U.S. custody is not the work of a few "bad apples." It is part of a systematic and official strategy by the Bush administration to circumvent the law and avoid criminal liability for it. All individuals, military and non-military, who played any role in the mistreatment of prisoners in U.S. custody should be prosecuted under the Torture Statute, the War Crimes Act, and all other pertinent U.S. laws. Commanders all the way up the chain of command who were responsible must not escape criminal prosecution.

Despite documentation of numerous instances of torture and abuse by individuals and groups of persons both in the U.S. Armed Forces and contractors or mercenaries employed by the military, only a handful of low-ranking enlisted men and officers have been prosecuted, none for torture or war crimes.

Former Specialist Charles A. Graner is serving a 10-year sentence for five charges of assault, maltreatment, and conspiracy committed during his tenure as a guard at Abu Ghraib.[5] Specialist Sabrina Harman, who forced the hooded, wired man onto the box seen around the world, was convicted of one count of conspiracy to maltreat detainees, four counts of maltreating detainees, and one count of dereliction of duty and sentenced to six months in custody.[6] Pfc. Lynndie R. England, who posed with the pyramid of naked detainees, was convicted of one count of conspiracy, four counts of maltreating detainees, and one count of committing an indecent act;[7] she was sentenced to three years in prison.[8] Four other Abu Ghraib guards accepted plea agreements and received sentences ranging from no time to eight and a half years.[9]

Navy SEAL Lt. Andrew K. Ledford was acquitted of assault, making false official statements, dereliction of duty, and conduct unbecoming an officer at Abu Ghraib.[10] He was accused of joining his men as they beat a hooded, handcuffed Iraqi man, who died shortly after the SEALs handed him over to the Central Intelligence Agency (CIA). Eight SEALs and one sailor received administrative punishment for the incident.[11] A photograph of Manadel al-Jamadi's body, wrapped in plastic and packed in ice, became one of the most grotesque images to emerge from the Abu Ghraib scandal.[12] The ad hoc collaboration between the SEALs and the CIA came out at Ledford's trial. There were "several suggestions during the trial that the involvement of CIA or other American intelligence personnel appeared to contribute to the harsh treatment of some detainees by members of the Seals."[13] No homicide charges have been brought.[14]

Five years after two Afghans were found dead, hanged by their shackled wrists in isolation cells at the U.S. prison in Bagram, Afghanistan, the prosecution has faltered. Although Army investigators recommended criminal charges against 27 soldiers and officers, only 15 have been prosecuted. Five pled guilty to assault and other crimes, but the longest sentence any has received is five months in a military prison. One soldier was convicted at trial, but he was not imprisoned.[15]

"Despite a number of investigations," Human Rights Watch found in 2006, "the United States has not robustly prosecuted cases of alleged detainee abuse or homicide. In the majority of cases involving alleged abuse, military commanders have taken potential prosecutions before administrative hearing boards for non-judicial punishments, such as 'reprimands,' 'admonishments,' rank reductions, and discharges, instead of bringing them for criminal prosecution before courts martial."[16]

The rights organization also determined, "With civilians implicated in prisoner abuse, the record is even worse: despite extensive evidence that CIA personnel and civilian contractors were involved in several homicides, the DOJ [Department of Justice] has not prosecuted a single agent in a federal court for abuse, except for one CIA contractor, who was charged with assault in connection with a homicide in Afghanistan in 2003."[17] At the end of 2006, Congress decided that U.S. military contractors operating in combat zones would also be subject to the Uniform Code of Military Justice.

The Nuremberg Tribunal prescribed punishment not only for the persons who actually performed the acts, but it also provided that "Leaders, organizers, instigators and accomplices participating in the formulation or execution of a common plan or conspiracy to commit [war crimes] are responsible for all acts performed by any persons in the execution of such plan."[18]

The Bush gang engaged in a common plan to commit war crimes. In elaborate memoranda prepared for the President, his hired guns devised a scheme to violate our laws against torture and war crimes and get away with it.[19] In other words, the attorneys were accomplices in the commission of war crimes.

Alberto Gonzales advised Bush that the war on terror is a "new paradigm," so the President could suspend the Geneva Conventions because they were "quaint" and "obsolete." Where did Gonzales get these ideas? When Nazi leaders were on trial for war crimes after World War II, their lawyers argued that the Soviets were "barbaric" foes who engaged in nonconventional "terrorist" practices, and protections of the Geneva Conventions were thus "quaint" and "obsolete."[20] A striking coincidence.

Under the U.S. Army Field Manual,

[M]ilitary commanders may be responsible for war crimes committed by subordinate members of the armed forces, or other persons subject to their control. Thus, for instance, when troops commit massacres and atrocities against the civilian population of occupied territory or against prisoners of war, the responsibility may rest not only with the actual perpetrators but also with the commander. Such a responsibility arises directly when the acts in question have been committed in pursuance of an order of the commander concerned. The commander is also responsible if he has actual knowledge, or should have knowledge, through reports received by him or through other means, that troops or other persons subject to his control are about to commit or have committed a war crime and he fails to take the necessary and reasonable steps to insure compliance with the law of war or to punish violators thereof.[21]

In November 2005, Lawrence Wilkerson, Colin Powell's chief of staff, charged on National Public Radio that the policies on the treatment of prisoners that emanated from Dick Cheney's office triggered the abuse and torture. "It was clear to me that there was a visible audit trail that ran from the Vice-President's office through the Secretary of Defense down to the commanders in the field," Wilkerson said.[22]

The Schlesinger Report found: "Although the most egregious instances of detainee abuse were caused by the aberrant behavior of a limited number of soldiers and the predilections of the non-commissioned officers . . . Military and civilian leaders at the Department of Defense share this burden of responsibility."[23]

Human Rights Watch called for an investigation of Donald Rumsfeld, former CIA Director George Tenet, Lt. Gen. Ricardo Sanchez, Maj. Gen. Geoffrey Miller, and other generals in Iraq for war crimes and torture.[24] Its 2005 report says:

> Secretary Rumsfeld should be investigated for war crimes and torture by U.S. troops in Afghanistan, Iraq, and Guantánamo under the doctrine of "command responsibility." Secretary Rumsfeld created the conditions for U.S. troops to commit war crimes and torture by sidelining and disparaging the Geneva Conventions, by approving interrogation tech-

niques that violated the Geneva Conventions as well as the Convention against Torture, and by approving the hiding of detainees from the International Committee of the Red Cross. From the earliest days of the war in Afghanistan, Secretary Rumsfeld was on notice through briefings, ICRC reports, human rights reports, and press accounts that U.S. troops were committing war crimes, including acts of torture. However, there is no evidence that he ever exerted his authority and warned that the mistreatment of prisoners must stop. Had he done so, many of the crimes committed by U.S. forces could have been avoided.[25]

Its "World Report 2006" charges that torture and mistreatment have been a deliberate part of the Bush administration's counterterrorism strategy, undermining the global defense of human rights. Abusive interrogation, the rights organization determined, cannot be reduced to the misdeeds of a few low-ranking soldiers, but was a conscious policy choice by senior U.S. government officials. The report cites former CIA Director Porter Goss's defense of the torture technique of water-boarding as a "professional interrogation" technique. "Since 2002, over three hundred specific cases of serious detainee abuse have surfaced. At least eighty-six detainees have died in U.S. custody since 2002, and the U.S. government has admitted that at least twenty-seven of these cases were criminal homicides."[26]

General Taguba recommended that 12 officers at Abu Ghraib prison be reprimanded and many relieved from their duties. In April 2005, the Army Inspector General cleared four of the five top Army officers who oversaw prison policies and operations at Abu Ghraib. Lt. Gen. Ricardo Sanchez, who authorized the use of vicious dogs to exploit Arabs' fear of dogs, was exonerated, as was his deputy, Maj. Gen. Walter Wojdakowski. Col. Marc Warren, the command's top legal officer, who failed to report abuses witnessed by the International Committee of the Red

Cross (ICRC) to his boss for more than one month, escaped unscathed. And the report cleared Maj. Gen. Barbara Fast, former chief intelligence officer in charge of the Abu Ghraib intelligence center, who failed to advise Sanchez properly about the management of interrogations. In May 2005, the Army cited Col. Thomas M. Pappas for dereliction of duty, handed him a formal reprimand, and assessed a fine of $8,000 in an administrative proceeding. Pappas will not face criminal charges, according to two senior Pentagon officials.[27] Although a high-level military investigation recommended that Maj. Gen. Geoffrey Miller be reprimanded for his role in the mistreatment of prisoners at Guantánamo, a top Army general rejected the recommendation.[28]

Lt. Col. Steven Jordan, who ran Abu Ghraib's interrogation center, was finally charged, but not with war crimes. He is facing a possible 22 years in prison for cruelty and maltreatment of prisoners, disobeying a superior officer, willful dereliction of duty, and making false statements.[29] Former Brig. Gen. Janis L. Karpinski was the highest ranking officer to be demoted (to Colonel) and reprimanded.[30] Karpinski was not punished for the Abu Ghraib scandal, however. The reason given: shoplifting. Karpinski, who claimed the torture and abuse was hidden from her, was a scapegoat for the Bush administration.[31]

INTERNATIONAL PROSECUTIONS

At the Nuremberg Tribunal, individuals were held criminally liable for the first time for war crimes and crimes against humanity. Japanese leaders were also tried for atrocities committed during World War II. Yet U.S. leaders who were responsible for some of the most heinous war crimes ever committed—the atomic bombings of Hiroshima and Nagasaki and the fire bombings of Dresden, Tokyo, and more than 60 other Japanese cities—were never brought to justice. Only the vanquished

Germans and Japanese were put on trial. Justice Radhabinod Pal of India, dissenting at the Tokyo War Crimes Tribunal, called this "victor's justice." Indeed, Robert McNamara, who participated in the bombing of Japan during World War II, said in the film *Fog of War* that he and General Curtis LeMay would have been tried for war crimes if the United States had lost the war. McNamara admitted, "LeMay said if we lost the war that we would have all been prosecuted as war criminals. And I think he's right. He . . . and I'd say I . . . were behaving as war criminals."

The International Criminal Court (ICC), located in The Hague, is the product of 50 years of work by many countries to bring the perpetrators of the most heinous crimes to justice. Its statute, ratified by virtually every Western democracy except the United States, ensures an independent and impartial process. The court has jurisdiction to punish war crimes and crimes against humanity. Torture is considered both a war crime and a crime against humanity under the ICC statute.

Widespread or systematic torture and other inhumane acts against a civilian population that intentionally cause great suffering or serious mental or physical injury constitute crimes against humanity, including the targeting of and failure to protect civilians. The dropping of 2,000-pound bombs in residential areas of Baghdad during "Shock and Awe" was a crime against humanity. The indiscriminate U.S. attack on Fallujah, which was collective punishment in retaliation for the killing of four Blackwater mercenaries, was a crime against humanity. The destruction of hospitals in Fallujah by the U.S. military, its refusal to let doctors treat patients, and shooting into ambulances were crimes against humanity. Declaring Fallujah a "weapons-free" zone, with orders to shoot anything that moved, was a crime against humanity.

The ICC will prosecute offenses only if a country that has jurisdiction over the case is unwilling or unable to prosecute. The court can try citizens of countries (1) that are parties to the treaty, (2) on whose territory the conduct occurred, and (3) of which the accused is a national. Fearful that the Bush gang might become defendants in war crimes prosecutions, Bush renounced the ICC in May 2002. The United States has reportedly extracted from more than 100 countries bilateral immunity agreements that they will not extradite Americans who are indicted by the ICC to The Hague. The Bush administration punishes countries that refuse to sign these agreements by cutting off their foreign aid. In August 2002, Congress passed the American Servicemembers Protection Act of 2002[32] (known as the Hague Invasion Act), which authorizes the President to use any means necessary to secure the release of an American who is detained by or on behalf of the ICC. It also prohibits military assistance to countries that ratify the treaty.

Reacting to Bush's renunciation of the ICC, Yale law professor Bruce Ackerman wrote, "It is one thing to protect the armed forces from politicized justice; quite another, to make it a haven for suspected war criminals."[33] There are other avenues to bring the Bush gang to justice. Any country, including the United States, has the authority to prosecute any person for commission of the most heinous crimes under the principle of *universal jurisdiction*.[34] Israel used universal jurisdiction to prosecute, convict, and execute Adolph Eichmann for his crimes during the Holocaust, even though he and his crimes had no direct connection with Israel.

Although many have called for indictment of high officials of the Bush administration for war crimes, it is unlikely any country would risk the wrath of the U.S. government by initiating such a prosecution. For example, Belgium indicted George W. Bush, Tony Blair, former Deputy Secretary of Defense Paul

Wolfowitz, John Ashcroft, and Condoleezza Rice for war crimes committed during the U.S.-led military campaign in Afghanistan. Belgium's universal jurisdiction law gave Belgian courts the right to judge anyone accused of war crimes, crimes against humanity, or genocide, regardless of where the crimes were committed. Four Rwandans were convicted in 2001 under Belgian law for their participation in the 1994 genocide, which left more than one million dead. Rumsfeld threatened to move the North Atlantic Treaty Organization (NATO) out of Brussels unless Belgium changed its universal jurisdiction law. Belgium capitulated and dismissed the war crimes indictments.

On November 14, 2006, two Nobel Peace Prize laureates, the Center for Constitutional Rights (CCR), the National Lawyers Guild (NLG), and 24 other nongovernmental organizations from more than 15 countries asked the German federal prosecutor to initiate a criminal investigation into the war crimes of Donald Rumsfeld, George Tenet, Stephen Cambone, Ricardo Sanchez, Walter Wojdakowski, Geoffrey Miller, Thomas Pappas, Alberto Gonzales, Jay Byee, John Yoo, William Haynes, and David Addington. When the CCR filed a similar complaint in Germany two years before, the German prosecutor declined to investigate the U.S. officials because there was "no indication" that the United States wouldn't bring them to justice. In the interim, Congress passed the Military Commissions Act, immunizing these leaders from war crimes prosecutions. This is a definitive indication that the U.S. government will not prosecute them. On April 27, 2007, however, the German federal prosecutor dismissed the complaint.

LEGAL CHALLENGES TO THE NSA SPYING PROGRAM

Dozens of lawsuits were brought by groups—including CCR, NLG, the American Civil Liberties Union (ACLU), and the

Electronic Frontier Foundation—seeking to stop the NSA's eavesdropping program. The Bush administration argued that allowing the cases to proceed would force the government to reveal state secrets. U.S. District Court Chief Judge Vaughn Walker in San Francisco rejected that argument because Bush had already publicly affirmed the Terrorist Surveillance Program. Walker wrote, "The compromise between liberty and security remains a difficult one. But dismissing this case at the outset would sacrifice liberty for no apparent enhancement of security."[35] U.S. District Court Judge Anna Diggs Taylor in Detroit also refused to accept the government's state secrets defense. She decided that the NSA program violated the Foreign Intelligence Surveillance Act (FISA), the Fourth Amendment, the First Amendment, and the separation of powers doctrine. In her decision, Taylor charged, "There are no hereditary Kings in America and no powers not created by the Constitution."[36] The government's appeal was pending when we went to press.

As the Bush gang faced the judicial music for the NSA program, it suddenly did an about face. Shortly before the surveillance program was to be given its first appellate hearing, Alberto Gonzales announced that the administration decided to rely on the FISA court to approve their eavesdropping and Bush would not reauthorize his Terrorist Surveillance Program. But when challenged on the details, Bush remained vague, saying, "Nothing has changed in the program except the court has said we've analyzed it and it's a legitimate way to protect the country."[37]

MORE ATTACKS ON THE CONSTITUTION

During the January 18, 2007, Senate Judiciary Committee hearing on whether to reinstate the right to habeas corpus the Military Commissions Act purported to rescind, Gonzales made the astounding claim that "there is no express grant of habeas [corpus] in the Constitution. There is a prohibition against taking it away."[38] Gonzales' tortured logic could be used to claim there is no right to freedom of speech, press, or religion either given that the First Amendment reads, "Congress shall make no law . . . prohibiting the free exercise [of religion]; or abridging the freedom of speech, or of the press. . . ."

Deputy Assistant Secretary of Defense Charles "Cully" Stimson had just attacked the lawyers who have volunteered to represent the Guantánamo detainees. Flashing a list of corporations that use law firms doing this pro bono work, Stimson declared, "Corporate C.E.O.'s seeing this should ask firms to choose between lucrative retainers and representing terrorists." This was a not-so-veiled call for corporations to boycott law firms that represent detainees at Guantánamo.

A brief history lesson might help here. In 1770, John Adams defended nine British soldiers, including a captain who stood accused of killing five Americans. No other lawyer would defend them. Adams thought no one in a free country should be denied the right to a fair trial and the right to counsel. He was subjected to scorn and ridicule and claimed to have lost half his law practice as a result of his efforts. Adams later said his representation of those British soldiers was "one of the most gallant, generous, manly and disinterested actions of my whole life, and one of the best pieces of service I ever rendered my country."

U.S. District Court Judge Joyce Hens Green, who has handled the many habeas corpus petitions filed by the Guantánamo detainees, expressed appreciation for the lawyers: "I do want to say we are very grateful for those attorneys who have accepted pro bono appointments. That is a service to the country, a service to the parties. No matter what position you take on this, it is a grand service." The American Bar Association's Model Rules of Professional Conduct require every lawyer to "provide legal services to those unable to pay." Lawyers have a duty to represent the defenseless and the oppressed.

The Supreme Court held in *Rasul v. Bush* that the Guantánamo prison is under U.S. jurisdiction, so prisoners there are entitled to the protections of the Constitution. The Sixth Amendment mandates that every person charged with a crime has the right to be defended by an attorney. The government is forbidden by the Fifth Amendment from denying any "person," U.S. citizen or not, due process of law. The presumption of innocence is enshrined in our legal system.

After the NLG, the Association of American Jurists, the International Association of Democratic Lawyers, and the Society of American Law Teachers called for Stimson's ouster, he wrote a half-hearted apology in the *Washington Post*, and later resigned. Yet Stimson's threats against the corporate lawyers who volunteer to represent those caught in Guantánamo's black hole will continue to reverberate in the corporate board rooms.

STOP THE COWBOY REPUBLICANS

More than 3,000 American soldiers and hundreds of thousands of Iraqi civilians have died. Untold numbers have been wounded and maimed in Iraq. Our national debt has skyrocketed with the billions of dollars Bush has pumped into the war. The tab may well reach $2 trillion. There is much talk of pulling our troops out of Iraq. Why would Dick Cheney and the neocons who convinced Bush to start this war ever decide to withdraw? They created the war to achieve their imperial dream of privatizing Iraqi oilfields and building permanent U.S. military bases nearby to protect them. They have shown themselves willing to sacrifice the lives of our soldiers and the Iraqi people in pursuit of their dream.

Now that there's a new day in Congress, there must be a new

push to end the war. That means a demand that Congress cut off the funds. Although some legislators questioned their authority to stop the war, even the infamous John Yoo admitted Congress has that power. "It's perfectly constitutional and legal for Congress to cut off funds for any war it doesn't want the country to fight, and it's done that before," Yoo said, referring to Congress's cutoff of funds for Vietnam in 1973.[39] Although Congress did not have the votes to override a presidential veto, Richard Nixon refrained from vetoing the funding cut to avoid offending legislators who might vote to impeach him over the Watergate scandal.

Congress also has the authority to declare that Bush may not use military appropriations to alter the scope or nature of the conflict that Congress authorized and funded. This means prohibiting him from using appropriated funds to increase troop levels or to broaden the conflict into additional nations or territories.[40] Congress has a responsibility to prevent the Bush gang from attacking Iran. In view of congressional opposition to his war in Iraq, Bush will not likely ask permission to make war on Iran. He may try to bootstrap the September 2001 and October 2002 congressional authorizations for force into consent to attack Iran. We can expect Bush to provoke—or even fabricate—an incident with Iran and then claim he's responding to Iranian aggression. Congress has the power to prevent war with Iran; it remains to be seen whether it has the will.

Ultimately, it is up to the American people to step up to the plate and stop Bush's wars. It's fine to tell the pollsters we want our troops out of Iraq. That's not doing the trick. The Vietnam War ended after tens of thousands of people marched in the streets. We may not have the draft to get all of the college kids off their duffs, but we do have our consciences. And that should be enough.

The Congress and the American people should not succumb to the Bush gang's fear-mongering. In 1933, President Franklin D. Roosevelt said, "Let me assert my firm belief that the only thing we have to fear is fear itself—nameless, unreasoning, unjustified terror which paralyzes needed efforts to convert retreat into advance." We must also demand that the Guantánamo gulag be closed and call a halt to Bush's evisceration of our civil liberties under the guise of his "war on terror." Justice Thurgood Marshall once wrote, "History teaches that grave threats to liberty often come in times of urgency, when constitutional rights seem too extravagant to endure. The World War II relocation-camp cases—and the Red Scare and McCarthy era internal subversion cases—are only the most extreme reminders that when we allow fundamental freedoms to be sacrificed in the name of real or perceived exigency, we invariably come to regret it."[41]

Those who turn their heads because they think the cutbacks on civil liberties don't affect them should heed the words of Martin Niemoller, characterizing the "typical German" in the 1930s: "First they came for the Communists, but I was not a Communist, so I said nothing. Then they came for the Social Democrats, but I was not a Social Democrat, so I did nothing. Then came the trade unionists, but I was not a trade unionist. And then they came for the Jews, but I was not a Jew, so I did little. Then when they came for me, there was no one left who could stand up for me."[42] Bush's hubris affects us all.

Toward the end of the Vietnam War, Daniel Ellsberg leaked "The Pentagon Papers," which revealed the truth about that illegal and tragic war. Ellsberg has called on American officials to "leak more" but "in a timely way," which means right now. "Don't do what I did," he says. "Don't wait until the bombs are falling in Iran."

Many, including the NLG, have called for the impeachment

of Bush and Cheney for their high crimes and misdemeanors. Both Nancy Pelosi, the new Speaker of the House, and John Conyers, the incoming chairman of the House Judiciary Committee where impeachment would be initiated, have said, "Impeachment is off the table." But if Congress fulfills its constitutional duty to investigate the Bush gang's malfeasance, the legislators will invariably encounter stonewalling by the administration. That should anger many in Congress, who then might develop the resolve to launch impeachment proceedings.

Before George W. Bush invaded Iraq, 11 million people around the world took to the streets and opposed the war. The Bush administration will continue to prosecute its permanent wars on other countries while destroying our civil liberties to avoid dissent. It is now time for us to demand truth, justice, and accountability from the Cowboy Republicans. That means op-eds and letters to the editor, and writing, e-mailing, and calling Congress, insisting that the Bush gang be held to account for its high crimes and misdemeanors. We must organize protests, marches, and demonstrations to end the Iraq war and occupation now and prevent the next war. Our lives and those of our children depend on it.

Notes

CHAPTER 1

1. Ron Suskind, *The Price of Loyalty: George W. Bush, the White House, and the Education of Paul O'Neill* (New York: Simon & Shuster, 2004), 129.

2. Stephen C. Schlesinger, *Act of Creation: The Founding of the United Nations—A Story of Superpowers, Secret Agents, Wartime Allies and Enemies, and Their Quest for a Peaceful World* (Boulder, CO: Westview, 2003), 289–94.

3. Project for the New American Century (PNAC), "Rebuilding America's Defenses: Strategy, Forces and Resources for a New Century" (Sept. 2000), 63. http://www.newamericancentury.org/Rebuilding AmericasDefenses.pdf.

4. Judicial Watch, "Maps and Charts of Iraqi Oilfields." http://www.judicialwatch.org/iraqi-oil-maps.shtml.

5. See note 3.

6. Although beyond the scope of this book, "Operation Enduring Freedom" in Afghanistan was illegal because it was neither executed in self-defense, nor authorized by the Security Council. Although the Taliban hosted terrorist training camps and harbored al-Qaeda leader Osama bin Laden, Afghanistan never attacked the United States. The two relevant Security Council resolutions end by deciding that the Council will "remain seized of the matter," which means the Council retains jurisdiction over the situation. Neither resolution grants the United States or any country permission to attack Afghanistan.

7. William Rivers Pitt and Scott Ritter, *War on Iraq: What Team Bush Doesn't Want You to Know* (New York: Context Books, 2002), 29.

8. Nelson Mandela, "The U.S.A. Is a Threat to World Peace," *Newsweek,* Sept. 10, 2002. http://msnbc.msn.com/id/3070095/.

9. Letter dated 16 September 2002 from the Minister of Foreign Affairs of Iraq addressed to the Secretary-General, S/2002/1034. http://www.un.org/Depts/unmovic/chronology/1034.pdf#search=%2 2Naji%20Sabri%20September%2016%22.

10. Bob Woodward, *Plan of Attack* (New York: Simon & Schuster, 2004), 253; Frank Rich, "The Ides of March 2003," *New York Times,* Mar. 19, 2007, 7.

11. Greg Miller, "Analysis of Iraqi Weapons 'Wrong'—The Predicted Use of Banned Agents Did Not Occur, a Marine Commander Says: The CIA Chief Defends His Staff's Assessments," *Los Angeles Times,* May 31, 2003, 1.

12. Julian Borger, "Threat of War: U.S. Intelligence Questions Bush Claims on Iraq," *Guardian,* Oct. 9, 2002, 12.

13. "CNN Presents: Dead Wrong" (CNN television broadcast, Aug. 21, 2005) (statement of Michael Scheuer).

14. "Truth, War & Consequences" (*Frontline,* PBS television broadcast, Aug. 12, 2003).

15. Bryan Burrough, Eugenia Peretz, David Rose, and David Wise, "The Path to War," *Vanity Fair,* May 2004, 204 (quoting Greg Thielmann).

16. Final Investigative Report Prepared at the Direction of Rep. John Conyers, Jr., "The Constitution in Crisis—The Downing Street Minutes and Deception, Manipulation, Torture, Retribution, Cover-ups in the Iraq War, and Illegal Domestic Surveillance," Aug. 2002. http://www.truthout.org/3.122005ConRes.pdf.

17. Ibid.

18. Ibid.

19. Murray Waas, "Key Bush Intelligence Brief Kept From Hill Panel," *National Journal,* Nov. 22, 2005. http://nationaljournal.com/about/njweekly/stories/2005/1122nj1.htm#.

20. "Report of the Select Committee on Intelligence on Postwar Findings About Iraq's WMD Programs and Links to Terrorism and How They Compare With Prewar Assessments Together with Addi-

tional Views," 109th Congress, Second Session, Sept. 8, 2002. http://
intelligence.senate.gov/phaseiiaccuracy.pdf; Jonathan Weisman, "Iraq's
Alleged Al-Qaeda Ties Were Disputed Before War," *Washington Post,*
Sep. 9, 2002, A01.

21. Report of the Select Committee on Intelligence. Walter Pincus, "CIA Learned in '02 That Bin Laden Had No Iraq Ties, Report
Says," *Washington Post,* Sept. 15, 2006, A14.

22. Ibid.

23. Douglas Jehl, "Report Warned Bush Team About Intelligence
Doubts," *New York Times,* Nov. 6, 2005, 114.

24. Michael Hirsh, John Berry, and Daniel Klaidman, "A Tortured
Debate: Amid Feuding and Turf Battles, Lawyers in the White House
Discussed Specific Terror-Interrogation Techniques Like 'Water
Boarding' and 'Mock Burials', *Newsweek,* June 21, 2004, 50.

25. See chapter 2.

26. See note 23; Ken Guide, "They Got What They Wanted: The
Folly of the Bush Administration's Torture Policy," *Center for American
Progress,* Aug. 5, 2004. http://www.americanprogress.org/issues/2004/
08/b134740.html; *Intelligence: More Proof Than They Knew,* July 15,
2004, http://www.americanprogress.org/site/pp.asp?c=biJRJ8OVF&b
=122149.

27. *60 Minutes* (CBS television broadcast, Jan. 11, 2004). http://
www.cbsnews.com/stories/2004/01/09/60minutes/main592330
.shtml.

28. Bob Woodward, *Bush at War* (New York: Simon and Schuster,
2002), 74, 84.

29. National Commission on Terrorist Attacks Upon the United
States, *The 9/11 Commission Report,* n. 75 (2004), 559–60. http://
www.9-11commission.gov/report/911Report.pdf.

30. "Interview with Bob Woodward," (*60 Minutes,* CBS television
broadcast, Apr. 18, 2004).

31. James Bamford, *A Pretext for War* (Garden City, NY: Double-
day, 2004), 333.

32. President George W. Bush, State of the Union Address (Jan.
29, 2002). http://www.whitehouse.gov/news/releases/2002/01/2002
0129-11.html.

33. See note 16.

34. Daniel Eisenberg, "We're Taking Him Out," *Time,* May 13, 2002, 36.

35. George Packer, *The Assassins' Gate* (New York: Farrar, Straus & Giroux, 2005), 45.

36. Eric Schmitt, "U.S. Plan for Iraq is Said to Include Attack on 3 Sides," *New York Times,* July 5, 2002, A1.

37. Michael Smith, "British Bombing Raids Were Illegal, Says Foreign Office," *Sunday Times,* June 19, 2005, 7.

38. Michael Smith, "RAF Bombing Raids Tried to Goad Saddam into War," *Sunday Times,* May 29, 2005, 2.

39. Democratic Hearing on the Downing Street Minutes, Before the H. Comm. on the Judiciary, 109th Cong. (2005) (testimony of Ray McGovern).

40. Michael Smith, "General Admits to Secret Air War," *Sunday Times,* June 26, 2005, 2.

41. Patrick J. Buchanan, *The Cheney Doctrine: War Without End,* Sept. 2, 2002. http://www.theamericancause.org/patarchives.html.

42. Frank Rich, "It's Bush-Cheney, Not Rove-Libby," *New York Times,* Oct. 16, 2005, 12; Elisabeth Bumiller, "Traces of Terror: The Strategy; Bush Aides Set Strategy to Sell Policy on Iraq," *New York Times,* Sept. 7, 2002, A1.

43. Michael Smith, "Blair Planned Iraq War From Start," *Sunday Times,* May 1, 2005, 7.

44. See note 42.

45. "Top Bush Officials Push Case Against Saddam," (CNN television broadcast, Sept. 8, 2002). http://archives.cnn.com/2002/ALLPOLITICS/09/08/iraq.debate.

46. President George W. Bush, "Remarks to the Nation on the Anniversary of Terrorist Attacks (Sept. 11, 2002)." http://www.whitehouse.gov/news/releases/2002/09/20020911-3.html.

47. President George W. Bush, "Remarks at the UN General Assembly (Sept. 12, 2002)." http://www.whitehouse.gov/news/releases/2002/09/20020912-1.html.

48. "President Bush Outlines Iraqi Threat, Remarks by the President on Iraq," Cincinnati Museum Center - Cincinnati Union Terminal, Cincinnati, Ohio, Oct. 7, 2002. http://www.whitehouse.gov/news/releases/2002/10/20021007-8.html.

49. Authorization for Use of Military Force against Iraq Resolution of 2002 ("AUMF"), 116 STAT. 1498, Public Law 107-243, Oct. 16, 2002, http://frwebgate.access.gpo.gov/cgi-bin/getdoc.cgi?dbname =107_cong_public_laws&docid=f:publ243.107.pdf.

50. Frank Rich, *The Greatest Story Ever Sold—The Decline and Fall of Truth From 9/11 to Katrina*, (New York: Penguin, 2006), 58 (citing Lloyd Grove, "The Reliable Source," *Washington Post*, July 19, 2003, A19. The adoption of the Military Commissions Act of 2006 a month before the 2006 midterm election followed the same script. (See chapter 4.)

51. See note 49.

52. President George W. Bush, State of the Union Address (Jan. 28, 2003). http://www.whitehouse.gov/news/releases/2003/01/2003 0128-19.html.

53. See note 16.

54. Frank Rich, 62. See note 50.

55. Sam Tanenhaus, "Bush's Brain Trust," *Vanity Fair*, July 2003, 114.

56. Dana Milbank and Mike Allen, "U.S. Shifts Rhetoric on Its Goals In Iraq—New Emphasis: Middle East Stability," *Washington Post*, Aug. 1, 2003, A14

57. "It Would Be a Short War," (CBS News broadcast, Nov. 15, 2002). http://www.cbsnews.com/stories/2002/11/15/world/printable 529569.shtml.

58. President George W. Bush, State of the Union Address (Jan. 20, 2004). http://www.whitehouse.gov/news/releases/2004/01/2004 0120-7.html.

59. Peter Baker, "Bush Says U.S. Pullout Would Let Iraq Radicals Use Oil as a Weapon," *Washington Post*, Nov. 5, 2006, A6.

60. Patrick E. Tyler, "U.S. Strategy Plan Calls For Insuring No Rivals Develop," *New York Times*, Mar. 8, 1992, A1.

61. "Executive Briefing: The Bush Administration's Energy Plan," May 17, 2001. http://www.gcsi.ca/downloads/bushenergyplan.pdf.

62. See note 4.

63. See note 16.

64. See note 1.

65. Ibid.

66. Charter of the United Nations, June 26, 1945, 59 Stat. 1031, T.S. NO. 993, 3 Bevans 1153, 51.

67. *Caroline Case*, 29 BFSP 1137-8; 30 BFSP 19-6 (1837).

68. George W. Bush, Graduation Speech at West Point (June 1, 2002). http://www.whitehouse.gov/news/releases/2002/06/20020601-3.html.

69. The National Security Strategy, Sept. 2002. http://www.white house.gov/nsc/nss/2002/nss5.html.

70. When Yemen refused to capitulate, a U.S. diplomat told the Yemeni ambassador that it was "the most expensive 'no' vote you would ever cast." Indeed, the United States punished Yemen, the poorest country in the Arab world, by cutting off its entire U.S. foreign aid package of $70 million (Michael Ratner, Jennie Green, and Barbara Olshansky, *Against War With Iraq: An Anti-War Primer*, Center for Constitutional Rights, 2003, 18.)

71. S/RES/678 (1990).

72. S/RES/687 (1991).

73. S/RES/1154 (1998).

74. S/RES/1441 (2002).

75. "Joint Statement by China, France and Russia Interpreting UN Security Council Resolution 1441" (2002). http://www.staff.city.ac.uk/p.willetts/IRAQ/FRRSCHST.HTM.

76. See note 16.

77. Hans Blix, *Disarming Iraq* (New York: Pantheon, 2004), 86.

78. See note 10.

79. Bryan Burrough, Eugenia Peretz, David Rose, and David Wise, "The Path to War," *Vanity Fair*, May 2004, 290.

80. Mark Danner, "The Secret Way to War," *New York Review of Books* 10, June 9, 2005, 52.

81. Ewen MacAskill and Julian Borger, "Iraq War was Illegal and Breached U.N. Charter, Says Annan," *The Guardian (UK)*, Sept. 16, 2004.

82. Address of Hans Corell, Thomas Jefferson School of Law, San Diego, Nov. 14, 2006.

83. Oliver Burkeman and Julian Borger, "War Critics Astonished as U.S. Hawk Admits Invasion was Illegal," *Guardian*, Nov. 20, 2003, 4.

84. International Covenant on Civil and Political Rights, 999

U.N.T.S. 171, U.N. Doc. A/6316 (1966), *opened for signature* December 19, 1966 (*entered into force* Mar. 23, 1976).

85. Article VI of the U.S. Constitution provides: "This Constitution, and the Laws of the United States which shall be made in Pursuance thereof; and all Treaties made, or which shall be made, under the Authority of the United States, shall be the supreme Law of the Land; and the Judges in every State shall be bound thereby, any Thing in the Constitution or Laws of and State to the Contrary notwithstanding." U.S. CONST., art. VI, § 1, cl. 2.

86. See note 84, art. 1(2).

87. "Legal Consequences for States of the Continued Presence of South Africa in Namibia (South West Africa) Notwithstanding Security Council Resolution 276 (1970)," 1971 ICJ 16, 31–2 (June 21); Western Sahara, 1975 ICJ 12, 31–33 (Oct. 16); "Concerning the Frontier Dispute" (Burk. Faso v. Rep. of Mali), 1986 ICJ. 554, 566–7 (Dec. 22); "Concerning East Timor" (Port. v. Austl.), 1995 ICJ 90, 265–8 (June 30).

88. Michael R. Gordon, "Aerial Pounding Intended to Push Iraq's Government Toward Brink," *New York Times,* March 22, 2003, A1; John F. Burns, "A Staggering Blow Strikes at the Heart of the Iraqi Capital," *New York Times,* Mar. 22, 2003, A1.

89. Greg Miller, "Head of Joint Chiefs Defends Use of Cluster Bombs in Iraq. Myers Says Few Fell in Populated Areas, but Reports of Casualties from Duds Persist," *Los Angeles Times,* Apr. 26, 2003, at A8; Larry Johnson, "War's Unintended Effects. Use of Depleted Uranium Weapons Lingers as Health Concern. 'A Lot of People are Getting Sick, and Nobody Is Willing to Connect the Dots,'" *Seattle Post-Intelligencer,* Aug. 4, 2003, A1; Sara Flounders, "Iraqi Cities 'Hot' with Depleted Uranium: Dutch Worry About Depleted Uranium As Troops Enter Iraq," *Coastal Post Online* (Sept. 2003). http://www.coastalpost.com/03/09/11.htm; Scott Peterson, "Remains of Toxic Bullets Litter Iraq. The Monitor Finds High Levels of Radiation Left by US Armor-Piercing Shells," *Christian Science Monitor,* May 15, 2003, 01; James T. Cobb, "Indirect Fires in the Battle of Fallujah, Field Artillery, March–April 2005," 23–5, http://www.ringnebula.com/FieldArtillery_Mar Apr2005.htm.

90. "Q&A: White phosphorus. The Pentagon's Confirmation that

it Used White Phosphorus as a Weapon During Last Year's Offensive in the Iraqi City of Falluja Has Sparked Criticism" (BBC News television broadcast, Nov. 16, 2005). http://news.bbc.co.uk/2/hi/middle _east/4441902.stm; Mike Whitney, "Covering Up Napalm in Iraq," *ZNet,* June 28, 2005, http://www.zmag.org/content/showarticle.cfm ?SectionID=15&ItemID=8186.

91. Convention Relative to the Protection of Civilian Persons in Time of War, art. 147, Aug. 12, 1949, 6 *UST* 3516, 75 *UNTS* 287.

92. David Brown, "Study Claims Iraq's 'Excess' Death Toll Has Reached 655,000," *Washington Post,* Oct. 11, 2006, A12.

93. Tim Reid, "U.S. Rejects Iraq Torture Claim," *Times (UK),* Sept. 22, 2006, 47.

94. UN Assistance Mission for Iraq, Human Rights Report, 1 July–31 August, 2006. http://www.uniraq.org/documents/HR%20 Report%20July%20August%202006%20EN.pdf.

95. Kirk Semple, "Relentless Sectarian Violence in Baghdad Stalks Its Victims Even at the Morgues," *New York Times,* July 30, 2006, 14.

96. Associated Press, "Poll Finds Iraqis Back Attacks on U.S. Troops," *Los Angeles Times,* Sept. 28, 2006, 8.

97. Declassified Key Judgments of the National Intelligence Estimate, "Trends in Global Terrorism: Implications for the United States," April 2006. http://www.nytimes.com/packages/html/politics/ nie20060926.pdf; Mark Mazzetti, "Backing Policy, President Issues Terror Estimate," *New York Times,* Sept. 27, 2006, A1.

98. "Interview with Pervez Musharraf," *The Daily Show with Jon Stewart* (The Comedy Channel television broadcast, Sept. 26, 2006). http://www.comedycentral.com/sitewide/media_player/play.jhtml ?itemId=75877.

99. Nuremberg Trial Proceedings Vol. 1, Charter of the International Military Tribunal, Art. 6 (a).

100. Justice Robert Jackson, Opening Statement before the International Military Tribunal, Nov. 21, 1945, http://www.roberthjackson .org/Man/theman2-7-8-1/.

101. *War Crimes and the American Conscience* (Erwin Knoll and Judith Nies McFadden eds., 1970), 1.

102. *The Trial of German Major War Criminals: Proceedings of the International Military Tribunal Sitting at Nuremburg Germany,* vol.

22, 426 (1950). http://www.yale.edu/lawweb/avalon/imt/proc/09-30-46.htm.

103. Benjamin B. Ferencz, *Tribute to Nuremberg Prosecutor Jackson.* http://www.benferencz.org/arts/79.html.

CHAPTER 2

1. Vice President Dick Cheney, *Meet the Press* (NBC news television broadcast, Sept. 16, 2001). http://www.pbs.org/wgbh/pages/frontline/darkside/etc/script.html.

2. John Barry, Michael Hirsh, and Michael Isikoff, "The Roots of Torture: The Road to Abu Ghraib Began After 9/11, When Washington Wrote New Rules to Fight a New Kind of War," *Newsweek,* May 24, 2004, 26.

3. War Crimes Act, 18 U.S.C. § 2441 (1996); Torture Convention Implementation Act of 1994, 18 U.S.C. § 2340–2340B.

4. Convention Against Torture and Other Cruel, Inhuman or Degrading Treatment or Punishment, Apr. 18, 1988, S. Treaty Doc. No. 100-20, 1465 UNTS. 85, article 2(2) [hereinafter Torture Convention]. See also International Covenant on Civil and Political Rights, Oct. 5, 1977, 148 Cong. Rec. S4781-84 (1992), 999 U.N.T.S. 171, [hereinafter ICCPR].

5. George W. Bush, "Statement by the President: United Nations International Day in Support of Victims of Torture" (June 26, 2003). http://www.whitehouse.gov/news/releases/2003/06/20030626-3.html.

6. Jane Mayer, "Outsourcing Torture," *New Yorker,* Feb. 14, 2005, 106.

7. Dana Milbank, "U.S. Tries to Calm Furor Caused by Photos. Bush Vows Punishment for Abuse of Prisoners," *Washington Post,* May 1, 2004, A01.

8. Barbara Slavin, "Abuse of Detainees Undercuts U.S. Authority, 9/11 Panel Says," *USA Today,* Nov. 15, 2005, 8A.

9. Inter-American Commission on Human Rights, Detainees at Guantanamo Bay, Cuba, Mar. 12, 2002, http://www.photius.com/rogue_nations/guantanamo.html. U.N. Econ. & Soc. Council [ECOSOC], Comm. On Human Rights, "Situation of Detainees at Guantánamo Bay," UN Doc. E/CN.4/2006/120, Feb. 15, 2006 (Leila Zerrougui, Leandro Despouy, Manfred Nowak, Asma Jahangir, and

Paul Hunt). Foreign Affairs Committee, *Human Rights Annual Report* 2005, 2004-05, HC 574, http://www.publications.parliament.uk/pa/cm200506/cmselect/cmfaff/574/57402.htm.

10. Carol J. Williams, "Marine Corps Issues Gag Order in Detainee Abuse Case," *Los Angeles Times,* Oct. 15, 2006, 24.

11. Ibid.

12. Torture Convention, article 1.

13. Cited in Mark Danner, *Torture and Truth* (New York Review of Books, 2004), 83–4.

14. Barry et al., 26, 31.

15. Danner, 88–89.

16. Danner, 105–6.

17. Danner, 115–66.

18. José E. Alvarez, "Torturing the Law," 37 *Case W. Res. J Int'l L.* 2005, 175–193.

19. See Michael Hirsh, John Barry, and Daniel Klaidman, "A Tortured Debate Amid Feuding and Turf Battles, Lawyers in the White House Discussed Specific Terror-Interrogation Techniques Like 'Water-Boarding' and 'Mock Burials,'" *Newsweek,* June 21, 2004, 50.

20. Eric Lichtblau, "Gonzales Speaks Against Torture During Hearing," *New York Times,* Jan. 7, 2005, A1.

21. Seymour Hersh, *Chain of Command: The Road from 9/11 to Abu Ghraib* (New York: HarperCollins, 2004), 2.

22. Charlie Savage, "Documents Link Rumsfeld to Prisoner's Interrogation," *Boston Globe,* Apr. 15, 2006, A1.

23. Jane Mayer, "The Memo," *New Yorker,* Feb. 27, 2006, 35. http://www.newyorker.com/fact/content/articles/060227fa_fact.

24. Jerald Phifer, Memorandum for Commander, Joint Task Force 170, Request for Approval of Counter-Resistance Strategies (Oct. 11, 2002). http://www.yirmeyahureview.com/archive/documents/prisoner_abuse/dod_sc_021011.pdf. Diane E. Beaver, Memorandum for Commander Joint Task Force 170, *Legal Review of Aggressive Interrogation Techniques* (Oct. 11, 2002), http://www.yirmeyahureview.com/archive/documents/prisoner_abuse/dod_sc_021011.pdf; William J. Haynes II, Action Memo, Counter-Resistance Techniques (Nov. 27,

2002), http://www.npr.org/documents/2004/dod_prisoners/200406 22doc5.pdf.

25. Alberto J. Mora, Statement for the Record: Office of General Counsel Involvement in Interrogation Issues, Memorandum for Inspector General, Department of the Navy, NAVIG Memo 5021 Ser 00/07 of 18 June 04, 3. http://www.newyorker.com/images/pdfs/mora memo.pdf.

26. Rumsfeld, Donald, Memorandum for the General Counsel of the Department of Defense, January 15, 2003, http://www.npr.org/ documents/2004/dod_prisoners/20040622doc6.pdf.

27. Danner, 183.

28. Ibid., 444.

29. Esther Schrader and Greg Miller, "U.S. Officials Defend Interrogation Tactics," *Los Angeles Times,* May 13, 2004, A11. "Mr. Kerry on Prisoners," *Washington Post,* Oct. 20, 2004, A26.

30. Jack Goldsmith, Memorandum to William H. Taft IV, et al., Regarding Draft Memorandum for Alberto R. Gonzales, Counsel to the President, Re. Permissibility of Relocating Certain "Protected Persons" from Occupied Iraq, 2–5, 14 (Mar. 19, 2004).

31. Barry et al., 26.

32. Human Rights Watch, "Leadership Failure, Firsthand Accounts of Torture of Iraqi Detainees by the U.S. Army's 82nd Airborne Division," Sept. 2005, Vol. 17, No. 3(G), http://hrw.org/reports/ 2005/us0905/. *See also* Richard A. Serrano, "More Iraqis Tortured, Officer Says," *Los Angeles Times,* Sept. 24, 2005, at 1.

33. Human Rights Watch, "Leadership Failure, Firsthand Accounts of Torture of Iraqi Detainees by the U.S. Army's 82nd Airborne Division," Sept. 2005, Vol. 17, No. 3(G), http://hrw.org/reports/ 2005/us0905/

34. President's Statement on Signing of H.R. 2863, the "Department of Defense, Emergency Supplemental Appropriations to Address Hurricanes in the Gulf of Mexico, and Pandemic Influenza Act, 2006," Dec. 30, 2005. http://www.whitehouse.gov/news/releases/ 2005/12/20051230-8.html.

35. Department of Defense Directive, "DoD Intelligence Interrogations, Detainee Debriefings, and Tactical Questioning," No. 3115.09,

Nov. 3, 2005. http://www.dtic.mil/whs/directives/corres/pdf/d311509 _110305/d311509p.pdf (emphasis added).

36. Ron Suskind, *The One Percent Doctrine: Deep Inside America's Pursuit of Its Enemies Since 9/11,* (New York: Simon & Schuster, 2006), 99–101, 115, 207.

37. Ibid., 115–6.

38. Report of the International Committee of the Red Cross (ICRC) on the Treatment by the Coalition Forces of Prisoners of War and Other Protected Persons by the Geneva Conventions in Iraq During Arrest, Internment and Interrogations, in Danner, 251–75.

39. Danner, 292.

40. Ibid., 292–3.

41. Ibid., 326.

42. Ibid., 337.

43. Ibid., 445.

44. U.N. Commission on Human Rights, "Report of Feb. 16, 2006, Regarding the Situation of Detainees at Guantánamo Bay." http://www.ohchr.org/english/bodies/chr/docs/62chr/E.CN.4.2006.1 20_.pdf; *See also* Sam Cage, "UN Calls Guantánamo a US Torture Camp,"Associated Press, Feb. 16, 2006.

45. Neil A. Lewis, "Widespread Hunger Strike at Guantánamo," *New York Times,* Sept. 18, 2005, 124.

46. Supplemental Declaration by Julia Tarver, *Esq, Majid Abdulla Al Joudi, et al. v. George W. Bush, et al.,* U.S. Dis. Ct. (D.C. Cir.), Civ. Action No. 05-0301 (GK), Oct. 13, 2005. All subsequent quotations are from this source.

47. UN Commission on Human Rights Report, 26.

48. Hernan Reyes, "Medical and Ethical Aspects of Hunger Strikes in Custody and the Issue of Torture," International Committee of the Red Cross, Jan. 1, 1998. http://www.icrc.org/Web/Eng/siteeng0.nsf/ iwpList302/F18AA3CE47E5A98BC1256B66005D6E29.

49. UN Commission on Human Rights Report, 39.

50. Ibid., 5–6.

51. Human Rights Watch, "United States Getting Away with Torture? A World of Abuse," 2005, http://www.hrw.org/reports/2005/ us0405/4.htm#_Toc101408092.htm.

52. Margaret Satterthwaite, Amnesty International, "Transferred to Torture," Sept. 12, 2006. http://www.alternet.org/story/41490.

53. Torture Convention, article 3.

54. Jon Boyle, "US 'Outsourced' Torture, European Investigator Says," Reuters, Jan. 24, 2006.

55. ACLU, Extraordinary Rendition—FACT Sheet, http://www.aclu.org/safefree/extraordinaryrendition/22203res20051206.html.

56. Douglas Jehl and David Johnston, "Rule Change Lets C.I.A. Freely Send Suspects Abroad to Jails," *New York Times,* Mar. 6, 2005, 1.

57. Human Rights Watch, "United States Getting Away with Torture? A World of Abuse," note 221.

58. Jane Mayer, *Outsourcing Torture,* note 6.

59. Ian Austen, "Canadians Fault U.S. for Its Role in Torture Case," *New York Times,* Sept. 19, 2006, A1.

60. Tracy Wilkinson, "Italy Orders Arrest of 13 CIA Operatives. Prosecutors Accuse the Americans of Taking Part in a Kidnapping: The 'Extraordinary Rendition' of a Terrorism Suspect to Egypt," *Los Angeles Times,* June 25, 2005, A1.

61. Mark Landler, "German Court Challenges CIA Over Abduction. Issues Warrants for 13. Case of Mistaken Arrest Puts Spotlight on Policy of Secret Transfers," *New York Times,* Feb. 1, 2007, A1.

62. *See* Human Rights Watch, "Developments Regarding Diplomatic Assurances Since April 2004," http://hrw.org/reports/2005/eca0405/5.htm.

63. Jane Mayer, "The Memo," *New Yorker,* Feb. 27, 2006. http://www.newyorker.com/fact/content/articles/060227fa_fact.

64. Rochin v. California, 342 U.S. 165, 172–74 (1952); Jackson v. Denno, 378 U.S. 368, 385–86 (1964). *See also* In re Guantánamo Detainee Cases, 355 F. Supp. 2d 443, 472–73 (DDC 2005).

65. Headquarters, U.S. Dept. of the Army, *Intelligence Interrogation,* FM 34-52, 108 (1992).

66. See note 6.

CHAPTER 3

1. Greg Miller and Josh Meyer, "CIA Missile in Yemen Kills 6 Terror Suspects. Unmanned plane fires at car carrying alleged Al Qaeda

operatives, Marking an Aggressive Shift in the Bush Administration's Tactics," *Los Angeles Times,* Nov. 5, 2002, A1.

2. Doug Cassel, "A Shot in the Dark, It's a Crime," *Chicago Tribune,* Feb. 2, 2003, 1.

3. President George W. Bush, State of the Union Address, Jan. 28, 2003. http://www.whitehouse.gov/news/releases/2003/01/20030128-19 .html.

4. U.N. Econ. and Soc. Council [ECOSOC], Report of the Special Rapporteur, Mr. Bacre Waly Ndiaye submitted pursuant to Commission on Human Rights resolution 1997/61: "Question of the Violation of Human Rights and Fundamental Freedoms in Any Part of the World, With Particular Reference to Colonial and Other Dependent Countries and Territories. Extrajudicial, Summary or Arbitrary Executions," E/CN.4/1998/68/Add.2 (Mar. 12, 1998).

5. See note 2.

6. Michel Chossudovsky, Centre for Research on Globalisation, "CIA Targeted Assassinations," Dec. 7, 2001, http://www.global research.ca/articles/NSA112A.html.

7. Seymour Hersh, *Chain of Command: The Road From 9/11 to Abu Ghraib* (New York: HarperCollins, 2004), 16.

8. Robert H. Jackson, *The Nürnberg Case* (New York: Alfred A. Knopf, 1947), 7-8.

9. Robert H. Jackson Center, *The Life of Robert H. Jackson,* http:// www.roberthjackson.org/Man/.

10. Kevin Sites, *Street by Street,* Nov. 10, 2004, http://www.kevin sites.net/2004_11_07_archive.html.

11. Convention Relative to the Protection of Civilian Persons in Time of War, art. 33, Aug. 12, 1949, 6 U.S.T. 3516, 75 UNTS 287.

12. Dahr Jamail and Ali Fadhil, "Rebuilding Not Yet Reality for Fallujah," Inter Press Service, June, 24, 2006, http://ipsnews.net/news .asp?idnews=33761.

13. Katarina Kratovac, "AP Photographer Flees Fallujah. Witnesses U.S. Helicopter Kill Fleeing Family of 5," Associated Press, Nov. 15, 2004, http://www.commondreams.org/headlines04/1115-04.htm. *See also* Katarina Kratovac, "AP photographer tells of his panicked flight from Fallujah raids," *St. Louis Post Dispatch,* Nov. 15, 2004, A08.

14. Kim Sengupta, "Witnesses Say US Forces Killed Unarmed

Civilians," *Independent (UK)*, Nov. 24, 2004, http://news.independent
.co.uk/world/middle_east/article21712.ece.

15. Anne Barnard, "Inside Fallujah's War: Empathy, Destruction
Mark a Week with U.S. troops," *Boston Globe*, Nov. 28, 2004, A1.

16. Kevin Sites, "Open Letter to Devil Dogs of the 3.1," Nov. 21,
2004, http://www.kevinsites.net/2004_11_21_archive.html.

17. "U.S. Investigates Falluja Killing. The U.S. Military Has
Announced It Is Looking into Whether an American Marine in Falluja
Shot Dead a Severely Wounded Iraqi Insurgent at Point-Blank Range,"
BBC News, Nov. 16, 2004, http://news.bbc.co.uk/go/pr/fr/-/1/hi/
world/middle_east/4014901.stm.

18. Rone Tempest, "Bloody Scenes Haunt a Marine. Member of
a Unit Under Investigation Recalls a Day in Iraq that Claimed a Buddy
and Civilians," *Los Angeles Times,* May 29, 2006, 1. http://www
.commondreams.org/cgi-bin/print.cgi?file=/headlines06/0529-04.htm.

19. Tony Perry and Julian E. Barnes, "Photos Indicate Civilians
Slain Execution-Style," *Los Angeles Times,* May 27, 2006, 1.

20. Richard A. Oppel, Jr., and Mona Mahmoud, "Iraqi's Accounts
Link Marines to the Mass Killing of Civilians," *New York Times*, May
29, 2006, A1.

21. Ellen Knickmeyer and Omar Fekeiki, "Baghdad Numb to
Reports of Massacre," *Washington Post,* May, 29, 2006, A19.

22. Ellen Knickmeyer, "Witnesses Recount Slayings of 24 in
Haditha," *Washington Post,* May 27, 2006 (no page) *available at* 2006
WLNR 9088648.

23. Ibid.

24. Kirk Mitchell, John Aloysius Farrell, Mike Soraghan, and Joey
Bunch, "No Direct Link Ties Marine to Deaths. Lt. Col. Jeffrey R.
Chessani of Rangely Lost His Post After His Unit Was Implicated in
Civilian Slayings, But Officials Say the Two Actions May Not Be Con-
nected," *Denver Post,* May 28, 2006, A01.

25. Jonathan Karl, "New Witness Describes Alleged Iraq Atrocity.
Girl, 12, Was Sole Survivor When Her Family Was Killed in Haditha;
Congressman Says 'Mass Murder' Was Covered Up," *ABC News,* ABC
television broadcast, May 28, 2006), http://abcnews.go.com/WNT/
print?id=2015052.

26. See note 20.

27. Tony Perry and Julian E. Barnes, "Photos Indicate Civilians Slain Execution Style. An official involved in an investigation of Camp Pendleton Marines' actions in an Iraqi town cites 'a total breakdown in morality,' *Los Angeles Times,* May 27, 2006, A1.

28. Paul Eckert, "Senator Vows Probe into Iraq Civilian Deaths," Reuters, May 28, 2006.

29. See note 18.

30. Thom Shanker, Eric Schmitt, and Richard A. Oppel, Jr., "Military to Report Marines Killed Iraqi Civilians," *New York Times,* May 26, 2006, A1. Robert H. Reid, "Analysis: Marine Scandal Could Roil Iraq," Associated Press, May 27, 2006.

31. "Gen. Batiste: 'Direct Link Between Haditha and Rumsfeld's "Bad Judgment,"'" June 4, 2006, http://thinkprogress.org/2006/06/04/batiste-haditha/.

32. See note 30.

33. Thomas E. Ricks, "Coverup of Iraq Incident By Marines Is Alleged," *Washington Post,* May 29, 2006, A19.

34. Douglass K. Daniel, "Murtha: Iraq Killings May Hurt War Effort," *Los Angeles Times,* May 28, 2006.

35. See note 20.

36. Ibid.

37. See note 30.

38. See note 22.

39. Nicholas Riccardi, "Interrogator Convicted in Iraqi's Death," *Los Angeles Times,* Jan. 22, 2006, A1. Josh White, "Documents Tell of Brutal Improvisation by GIs. Interrogated General's Sleeping-Bag Death, CIA's Use of Secret Iraqi Squad Are Among Details," *Washington Post,* Aug. 3, 2005, A01. Jim Trautman, "America's Woeful Record on Detainees," *Toronto Star,* Feb. 17, 2006, A21.

40. Paul Rockwell, "Army Reservist Witnesses War Crimes. New Revelations About Ongoing Brutality," *Online Journal,* April 2, 2005, http://www.informationclearinghouse.info/article8441.htm.

41. Convention Relative to the Protection of Civilian Persons in Time of War, article 49.

42. Bob Drogin, "Most 'Arrested By Mistake.' Coalition Intelligence Put Numbers at 70% to 90% of Iraq Prisoners, Says a February

Red Cross Report, Which Details Further Abuses," *Los Angeles Times,* May 11, 2004, 11.

43. Anne Hull, "Soldier Says He Was Doing His Duty When He Shot Civilian in Iraq," *Washington Post,* Sept. 24, 2006 (no page); *available at* 2006 WLNR 16570627.

44. Rory McCarthy, "'U.S. Soldiers Started to Shoot Us, One by One.' Survivors Describe Wedding Massacre as Generals Refuse to Apologize," *Guardian,* May 21, 2004, http://www.commondreams .org/headlines04/0521-01.htm.

45. Edward Wong, "G.I.'s Investigated in Slayings of 4 and Rape in Iraq," *New York Times,* July 1, 2006, A1. Raheem Salman and J. Michael Kennedy, "In Cold Blood; Iraqi Tells of Massacre at Farmhouse. A Cousin Describes Finding the Shot and Shattered Bodies. A U.S. Soldier Is in Custody," *Los Angeles Times,* July 6, 2006, 1. "Before Accusations, GI Described Killing Iraqis 'Like Squashing an Ant,'" *Agence France Press,* July 30, 2006, http://news.yahoo.com/s/afp/ 20060730/ts_alt_afp/iraqusmilitaryprobe.

46. Ellen Knickmeyer, "Iraqis Accuse Marines in April Killing of Civilian, *Washington Post Foreign Service,* June 5, 2006, A01; "7 Marines, Sailor Face Murder Charges: 8 to Be Charged in Death of Iraqi Civilian in April, Defense Lawyer Says," NBC News and News Services, June 1, 2006, http://www.msnbc.msn.com/id/13090111/ from/RS.3/print/1/displaymode/1098/.

47. Dahr Jamail, "Countless My Lai Massacres in Iraq," May 30, 2006, http://www.truthout.org/docs_2006/printer_053006Z.shtml.

48. Jim Wolf, "U.S. Troops Could Face Death Penalty in Iraq Case, Reuters, Sept. 3, 2006. Martin Bashir, "The 'Band of Brothers' Unravels," (*ABC News,* ABC television broadcast, Aug. 2, 2006), http://abcnews.go.com/Nightline/IraqCoverage/story?id=2265742& page=2.

49. Associated Press, "U.S. Army Charges Three With Murder in Iraq," June 19, 2006.

50. "Another Cover-Up? U.S. Troops Kill Two Iraqi Women, One of Them Pregnant, in Samarra," *Democracy Now!* (interview with Dahr Jamail), June 14, 2006, http://www.democracynow.org/print.pl?sid =06/06/14/1424235.

51. "Haditha Massacre: Was it an Isolated Event and Did the Military Try to Cover it Up?" *Democracy Now!* (interview with Matthew Shofield), May 30, 2006, http://www.democracynow.org/print.pl?sid =06/05/30/1332253.

52. Greg Mitchell, "Press Accounts Suggest Military 'Cover-up' in Isahqi Killings," *Editor & Publisher,* June 3, 2006.

53. Tim Golden, "Years After 2 Afghans Died, Abuse Case Falters," *New York Times,* Feb. 13, 2006, A1.

54. Jason Straziuso, "Karzai Orders Probe into U.S. Airstrike," Associated Press, May 23, 2006, 2006 WLNR 14796170.

55. Craig Pyes and Kevin Sack, "Firebase Gardez, A Times Investigation," *Los Angeles Times,* Sept. 25, 2006, 1.

56. Robert Fisk, "The Way Americans Like Their War," *Seattle Post-Intelligencer,* June 3, 2006, D4.

CHAPTER 4

1. Irene Khan, Speech at Foreign Press Association, May 25, 2005, http://web.amnesty.org/library/Index/ENGPOL100142005.

2. Statement of General Richard Myers (Jan. 11, 2002), http:// www.pbs.org/newshour/bb/asia/jan-june02/afghan_update_1-11 .html.

3. Joseph Margulies, *Guantánamo and the Abuse of Presidential Power* (New York: Simon & Schuster, 2006), 69.

4. Margulies, 226.

5. In 2003, the U.S. government admitted that children as young as 13 were being held at Guantánamo, and as of June 2005, there were reportedly nine prisoners at Guantánamo under the age of 18. The Convention on the Rights of the Child states that "every child deprived of his or her liberty shall have the right to prompt access to legal and other appropriate assistance, as well as the right to challenge the legality of the deprivation of his or her liberty before a court or other competent, independent and impartial authority, and to a prompt decision on any such action." (Convention on the Rights of the Child, G.A. Res. 44/25, UN GAOR, 44th Session, Annex 1, Supp. no. 49, 166, UN Doc. A/44/49 (1989) article 40) (*entered into force* Sept. 2, 1990). Even though the United States has not ratified the Convention on the

Rights of the Child, it is required, as a signatory, to refrain from action that would undermine the object and purpose of the treaty.

6. C. I. Beavans, ed. The Platt Amendment, *Treaties and Other International Agreements of the United States of America,* 1776–1949, vol. 8, (Washington, DC: United States Government Printing Office, 1971), article II, 1116–7.

7. Platt Amendment, article III.

8. Jonathan Wright, "Red Cross Criticizes U.S. for Guantánamo Bay Detentions," Reuters, Oct. 10, 2003. www.commondreams.org/headlines03/1010-08.htm.

9. Amnesty International, "United States of America. Holding Human Rights Hostage," Dec. 24, 2003. http://web.amnesty.org/library/Index/ENGAMR511642003.

10. Carol Leonnig, "Guantánamo Detainee Suing U.S. to Get Video of Alleged Torture," *Washington Post,* April 14, 2005, A02.

11. Nancy Gibbs with Viveca Novak, "Inside 'The Wire' Security Breaches. Suicidal Detainees. A Legal Challenge Heading to the Supreme Court. Welcome to Guantánamo," *Time,* Dec. 8, 2003, 40.

12. Mourad Benchellali, "Detainees in Despair," *New York Times,* June 14, 2006, A23.

13. Ben Knight, "Claims of Torture in Guantánamo Bay," Oct. 8, 2003. http://www.abc.net.au/am/content/2003/s962052.htm.

14. "U.S. Hands over Guantanamo Inmates. Seventeen Afghans Held in Guantánamo Bay Have Been Handed over to the Afghan Authorities in the Capital, Kabul," (*BBC News* television broadcast, Apr. 19, 2005). http://news.bbc.co.uk/2/hi/south_asia/4460603.stm.

15. Neil A. Lewis and Eric Schmitt, "Inquiry Finds Abuses at Guantánamo Bay," *New York Times,* May 1, 2005, 135.

16. Human Rights First, "Repeat Inquiry Finds Abuses at Guantánamo," *Law and Security News,* May 5, 2005, 45. http://www.humanrightsfirst.org/us_law/digest/usls_digest45_050505.htm.

17. Michele McPhee and Kimberly Atkins, "Say it ain't Mitt-mo; Hands off on Mass. Prisons, Governor to Advise on Guantánamo," *Boston Herald,* Apr. 21, 2006, 2.

18. See note 15.

19. Rasul v. Bush, 542 U.S. 466, 467-68 (2004); 28 USC §2241.

20. Hamdi v. Rumsfeld, 542 U.S. 507, 509, 516, 530, 532, 536 (2004).

21. Mark Denbeaux, Joshua Denbeaux, David Gratz, John Gregorek, Matthew Darby, Shana Edwards, Shane Hartman, Daniel Mann, Megan Sassaman, and Helen Skinner, "No-Hearings Hearings. CSRT: The Modern Habeas Corpus? An Analysis of the Proceedings of the Government's Combatant Status Review Tribunals at Guantánamo," Nov. 17, 2006. http://law.shu.edu/news/final_no_hearing _hearings_report.pdf.

22. Adam Liptak, "Detainee Deal Comes With Contradictions," *New York Times,* Sept. 23, 2006.

23. Amnesty International, "United States of America. The Threat of a Bad Example—Undermining International Standards as 'War on Terror' Detentions Continue," Aug. 19, 2003. http://web.amnesty .org/library/index/engamr511142003.

24. Detainee Treatment Act of 2005 is part of the Department of Defense Appropriations Act of 2006 (Title X, HR 2863).

25. Hamdan v. Rumsfeld, 126 S.Ct. 2749, 2759 (2006).

26. John O'Neil and Scott Shane, "High Court Blocks Guantánamo Trials. Ruling Represents a Decisive Rejection of Bush's Handling of Terror Suspects," *International Herald Tribune,* June 30, 2006, 1.

27. George W. Bush, "President Discusses Creation of Military Commissions to Try Suspected Terrorists," Sept. 6, 2006. http://www .whitehouse.gov/news/releases/2006/09/20060906-3.html; Adam Liptak, "Suspected Leader of Attacks on 9/11 Is Said to Confess," *New York Times,* Mar. 15, 2007.

28. Ibid.; Dana Priest, "CIA Holds Terror Suspects in Secret Prisons," *Washington Post,* Nov. 2, 2005, A1.

29. U.S. Const., article 1, §9(2) (the "Suspension Clause").

30. Abu Bakker Qassim, "The View From Guantánamo," *New York Times,* Sep. 17, 2006, 415.

31. *See* Bruce Ackerman, "Railroading Justice. Congress is Racing to Give the President the Power to Lock Up Almost Anyone," *San Diego Union-Tribune,* Sept. 28, 2006, B11.

32. Jane Sutton, "Guantánamo Illegal Despite Guilty Plea—Critics," Reuters, Mar. 28, 2007; William Glaberson, "Australian to Serve Nine Months in Terrorism Case," *New York Times,* Mar. 31, 2007, A10.

33. Somini Sengupta, "Guantánamo Comes to Define U.S. to Muslims," *New York Times,* May 21, 2005, A1.

34. Ibid.

35. "Tutu Calls for Guantánamo Closure. Archbishop Desmond Tutu Has Joined in the Growing Chorus of Condemnation of America's Guantánamo Bay Prison Camp" (*BBC News,* television broadcast, Feb. 17, 2006). http://news.bbc.co.uk/2/hi/americas/4723512.stm.

36. "U.N. report: U.S. Must Close Guantánamo," Associated Press, Feb. 16, 2006.

37. Committee Against Torture, "Consideration of Reports Submitted by States Parties Under Article 19 of the Convention," May 18, 2006, 36th session, CAT/C/USA/CO/2.

38. Ibid.

39. Caren Bohan, "Bush Acknowledges Guantanamo Damages U.S. Image," Reuters, June 14, 2006. http://www.truthout.org/docs _2006/061406S.shtml

40. "Military Plans to Build Compound for Trials," Associated Press, Nov. 18, 2006.

41. Carol Rosenberg, "Critics Assail Pentagon Plan for Terror Trials. Guantánamo Critics Reacted with Anger at the Pentagon's Plan to Build a Compound for War-Crimes Trials, Before the New Rules Are Announced and Any Civilian Court Challenges," *Miami Herald,* Nov. 18, 2006, A3.

42. Margulies, 214.

43. Abdullah Shihri, "Saudis Allege Torture in Guantánamo Deaths," Associated Press, June 11, 2006; Suzanne Goldenberg and Hugh Muir, "Killing Themselves Was Unnecessary. But it Certainly Is a Good PR Move," *Guardian (UK),* June 12, 2006. http://www .guardian.co.uk/guantanamo/story/0,,1795445,00.html.

44. Josh White, "Three Detainees Commit Suicide at Guantanamo," *Washington Post,* June 11, 2006, A01.

45. Goldenberg and Hugh Muir, note 43.

46. Andrew Selsky, "Suicides Renew Criticism of Guantánamo," Associated Press, June 1, 2006. http://www.mindfully.org/Reform/ 2006/Guantanamo-Colleen-Graffy11jun06.htm.

47. "Guantanamo Bay Hunger Strike Grows," Associated Press, June 1, 2006, http://www.cbsnews.com/stories/2006/06/01/terror/

main1674248.shtml; Onnesha Roychoudhuri, "Fatal Desperation at Guantanamo," June 13, 2006, http://www.alternet.org/story/37494/.

48. See note 46 and Roychoudhuri, note 47.

49. James Risen and Tim Golden, "Saudi Arabia Identifies 2 Dead Guantánamo Detainees," *New York Times,* June 11, 2006; see note 44.

CHAPTER 5

1. "Final Report of the Select Committee to Study Governmental Operations With Respect to Intelligence Activities," United States Senate, Apr. 26, 1976, http://www.icdc.com/~paulwolf/cointelpro/churchfinalreportIIb.htm ["Church Committee"].

2. James Risen and Eric Lichtblau, "Bush Lets U.S. Spy on Callers Without Courts," *New York Times,* Dec. 16, 2005, A1; President George W. Bush, "President's Radio Address," Dec. 17, 2005, http://www.whitehouse.gov/news/releases/2005/12/print/20051217.html; Attorney General Alberto Gonzales and Principal Deputy Director for National Intelligence General Michael Hayden, Press Briefing, Dec. 19, 2005, www.whitehouse.gov/news/releases/2005/12/20051219-1.html.

3. David E. Sanger and Eric Lichtblau, "Domestic Surveilance: The Issues; Administration Starts Weeklong Blitz in Defense of Eavesdropping Program," *New York Times,* Jan. 24, 2006, A18.

4. Barton Gellman, Dafna Linzer, and Carol D. Leonnig, "Surveillance Net Yields Few Suspects, *Washington Post,* Feb. 5, 2006, A1.

5. Senate Committee on the Judiciary, Foreign Intelligence Service Act of 1977, S. Rep. 95-604(I), reprinted in 1978 USCCAN 3904, 3909, 50 USC §1802 *et seq.*

6. Dorothy Ehrlich, "Taking Liberties: The Growing Scope of Government Power," *Los Angeles Daily Journal,* Feb. 26, 2002.

7. Senate Committee on the Judiciary, Foreign Intelligence Service Act of 1977, S.Rep. 95-604(I), reprinted in 1978 USCCAN 3904, 3909.

8. 50 USC §2511.

9. Foreign Intelligence Service Annual Report to Congress for the years 1979–2003, http://fas.org/irp/agency/doj/fisa.

10. President George W. Bush, speech given in Buffalo, NY, Apr. 20, 2004, http://www.areavoices.com/commonsense/?blog=1189.

11. James Risen and Eric Lichtblau, "Spying Program Snared U.S. Calls. Some Exchanges Are Said to Be Purely Domestic," *New York Times*, Dec. 21, 2005, A1.

12. Ibid.; Dan Eggen and Walter Pincus, "Campaign to Justify Spying Intensifies: NSA Effort Called Legal and Necessary, *Washington Post*, Jan. 24, 2006, A04.

13. Carol D. Leonnig, "Secret Court's Judges Were Warned About NSA Spy Data Program May Have Led Improperly to Warrants," *Washington Post*, Feb. 9, 2006, A1.

14. James Risen and Eric Lichtblau, "Bush Lets U.S. Spy on Callers without Courts," *New York Times*, Dec. 16, 2005, A1.

15. See note 13.

16. Carol D. Leonnig, "Surveillance Court is Seeking Answers," *Washington Post*, Jan. 5, 2006, A2.

17. Eric Lichtblau, "Judges on Secretive Panel Speak Out on Spy Program," *New York Times*, Mar. 29, 2006, A19.

18. Charlie Savage, "Specialists Doubt Legality of Wiretaps," *Boston Globe*, Feb. 2, 2006, A1.

19. "Presidential Authority to Conduct Warrantless Electronic Surveillance to Gather Foreign Intelligence Information," Congressional Research Service, Jan. 5, 2005, http://www.eff.org/Privacy/Surveillance/NSA/nsa_research_memo.pdf.

20. Editorial, "Ever-Expanding Secret," *New York Times*, May 12, 2006, A32.

21. United States v. United States District Court (Keith), 407 U.S. 297, 313-4, 317-8 (1972).

22. American Bar Association, Feb. 13, 2006, http://www.abanet.org/op/greco/memos/aba_house302-0206.pdf; National Lawyers Guild Condemns Electronic Surveillance by President as a Violation of the Fourth Amendment, Dec. 18, 2005, http://nlg.org/news/statements/electronicsurveillance2005.htm.

23. Transcript, "U.S. Senate Judiciary Committee Holds a Hearing on Wartime Executive Power and the NSA's Surveillance Authority," Feb. 6-7, 2006, http://www.washingtonpost.com/wp-dyn/content/article/2006/02/06/AR2006020600931.html.

24. Steven R. Weisman, "Powell Speaks Out on Domestic Spy Program," *New York Times*, Dec. 26, 2005, A1.

25. Authorization for Use of Military Force, Pub. Law 107-40, S.J. RES. 23, 107th Cong., Sep. 18, 2001.

26. Tom Daschle, "Power We Didn't Grant," *Washington Post,* Dec. 23, 2005, A21.

27. U.S. CONST., art. II, §3.

28. Youngstown Sheet & Tube Co. v. Sawyer, 343 U.S. 579, 637– 40 (1952).

29. Chitra Ragavan, "The Letter of the Law," *U.S. News & World Report,* Mar. 27, 2006, 27; Editorial, "This Call May Be Monitored . . . ," *New York Times,* Dec. 18, 2005, 411.

30. Scott Shane, "For Some, Spying Controversy Recalls a Past Drama," *New York Times,* Feb. 6, 2006, A18.

31. Leslie Cauley, "NSA Has Massive Database of Americans' Phone Calls," *USA Today,* May 11, 2006, A1.

32. Letter from Randal S. Milch, Senior Vice President and General Counsel at Verizon Business to Congressman John Conyers, Feb. 17, 2006; Letter from Marc Gary, Executive Vice President and General Counsel at Bell South to Congressman John Conyers, Apr. 4, 2006; Ken Belson and Matt Richtel, "Verizon Denies Yielding Local Phone Data," *New York Times,* May 17, 2006, A15; Arshad Mohammed, "BellSouth Wants Story Retractions," *Washington Post,* May 19, 2006, A7; Susan Page, "Lawmakers: NSA Database Incomplete, *USA Today,* June 30, 2006, 2A.

33. Eric Lichtblau and Scott Shane, "Bush Is Pressed Over New Report on Surveillance," *New York Times,* May 12, 2006, A1.

34. Seymour Hersh, "National Security Department, Listening In," *New Yorker,* May 29, 2006, 24.

35. 15 USC §78m(b)(3)(A).

36. 18 USC. §§3121, 3123 (2006); Anita Ramasastry, "The Recent Revelations About the NSA's Access to Our Phone Records: The Laws That Were Probably Broken, and the Likely Consequences," *Findlaw,* May 15, 2006, http://writ.news.findlaw.com/ramasastry/ 20060515.html.

37. Eric Lichblau and James Risen, "Bank Data Is Sifted in Secret by U.S. to Block Terror," *New York Times,* June 23, 2006, A1; *see also* Anita Ramasastry, "The Treasury Department's Secret Monitoring of

International Funds Transfers, *Findlaw,* http://technology.findlaw.com/articles/00006/010162.html.

38. Lowell Bergman, Eric Lichtblau, Scott Shane, and Don Van Natta, "Domestic Surveillance: The Program; Spy Agency Data After Sept. 11 Led F.B.I. to Dead Ends," *New York Times,* Jan. 17, 2006, A1.

39. Barton Gellman, Dafna Linzer, and Carol D. Leonnig, "Surveillance Net Yields Few Suspects," *Newsbyte,* 12:17:25, Feb. 5, 2006.

40. See note 38.

41. See note 12.

42. Bob Herbert, "Do You Know What They Know?" *New York Times,* Feb. 6, 2006, A27.

43. Charlie Savage, "On Eve of Hearing, Split on Spying: Some Prominent Conservatives Break with Bush," *Boston Globe,* Feb. 5, 2006, A1.

44. See note 23.

45. "National Lawyers Guild Condemns FBI's Operation Backfire as Unconstitutional," Dec. 12, 2006, http://www.nlg.org/news/statements/greenscare2006.htm.

46. Eric Lichtblau, "F.B.I. Watched Activist Groups, New Files Show," *New York Times,* Dec. 20, 2005, A1.

47. Lisa Myers, Douglas Pasternak, and Rich Gardella, "Is the Pentagon Spying on Americans?" MSNBC, Dec. 14, 2005, http://www.msnbc.msn.com/id/10454316; Michael Isikoff, "The Other Big Brother," *Newsweek,* Jan. 30, 2006, 32; Eric Lichtblau and Mark Mazzetti, "Military Documents Hold Tips on Antiwar Activities," *New York Times,* Nov. 21, 2006, A18.

48. The Attorney General's Guidelines, Mar. 17, 2003, http://www.epic.org/privacy/fbi/.

49. Neil A. Lewis, "Traces of Terror: The Inquiry. Ashcroft Permits FBI to Monitor Internet and Public Activities," *New York Times,* May 31, 2002, A20.

50. William Safire, "J. Edgar Mueller," *New York Times,* June 3, 2002, A15.

51. Eric Lichtblau, "FBI Scrutinizes Antiwar Rallies," *New York Times,* Nov. 23, 2003, 11.

52. Bob Barr, "The FBI's Pre-Emptive Interrogation of 'Possible'

Demonstrators: Chilling Political Speech," Aug. 24, 2004, *Findlaw,* http://writ.news.findlaw.com/commentary/20040825_barr.html.

53. Noah Leavitt, "Ashcroft's Subpoena Blitz. Targeting Lawyers, Universities, Peaceful Demonstrators, Hospitals, and Patients, All With No Connection to Terrorism," *Findlaw,* Feb. 18, 2004, http://writ.news.findlaw.com/commentary/20040218_leavitt.html.

54. See note 47.

55. Spencer S. Hsu, "FBI Papers Show Terror Inquiries into PETA; Other Groups Tracked," *Washington Post,* Dec. 20, 2005, A11.

56. Jonathan S. Landay, "FBI Documents Raise New Questions About Extent of Surveillance," Knight Ridder Washington Bureau, Mar. 14, 2006, *available at* 2006 WLNR 4270816; Dan Eggen, "FBI Took Photos of Anti-War Group in 2002," *Washington Post,* Mar. 15, 2006, *available at* 2006 WLNR 4272026.

57. Dan Eggen, "Possible FBI Violations in Eavesdropping Cited," *Washington Post,* Mar. 9, 2006, *available at* 2006 WLNR 3914616; "Justice Department Says FBI Misused Patriot Act," Associated Press, Mar. 9, 2007.

58. Douglas Birch, "NSA Used City Police as Trackers: Activists Monitored on Way to Fort Meade War Protest, Agency Memos Show," *Baltimore Sun,* Jan. 13, 2006, 1B.

59. *See* http://msnbcmedia.msn.com/i/msnbc/sections/news/DOD AntiWarProtestDatabaseTracker.pdf.

60. John Dean, "Why Should Anyone Worry about Whose Communications Bush and Cheney Are Intercepting, If It Helps to Find Terrorists?" *Findlaw,* Feb. 24, 2006, http://writ.news.findlaw.com/dean/20060224.html.

61. 277 U.S. 438, 479 (1928); Press Briefing by Ari Fleischer, Sep. 26, 2001, http://www.whitehouse.gov/news/releases/2001/09/20010926-5.html.

62. Chase Squires, "Gonzales Blasts Surveillance Critics," Associated Press (AP) Newswires 10:25:46, Nov. 19, 2006.

63. Frank Rich, "Will the Real Traitors Please Stand Up?" *New York Times,* May 14, 2006, 412.

64. Amy Goodman, "Is Bush Administration's Bank Spy Program One Part of a Resurgent Total Information Awareness?" *Democracy*

Now! June 27, 2006, http://www.democracynow.org/article.pl?sid=06/06/27/1433207.

65. Maura Reynolds, "Cheney Defends Domestic Spying," *Los Angeles Times*, Dec. 21, 2005, 20.

66. "Transcript of David Frost–Richard Nixon Interview," *New York Times*, May 20, 1977, A16.

67. John W. Dean, "An Update on President Bush's NSA Program: The Historical Context, Specter's Recent Bill and Feingold's Censure Motion," *FindLaw*, Mar. 24, 2006, http://writ.news.findlaw.com/dean/20060324.html.

68. Associated Press, "Ex-President Carter: Eavesdropping Illegal," Associated Press (AP) Newswires 00:40:53, Feb. 6, 2006.

69. John Nichols, "Frank Church and the Abyss of Warrantless Wiretapping," *Nation*, Apr. 26, 2006, http://www.thenation.com/blogs/thebeat?bid=1&pid=79968.

CHAPTER 6

1. J. Madison, *The Federalist* 1888, 47:300 (H. Lodge, ed.).

2. U.S. CONST., art. II, §3.

3. Clinton v. City of New York, 524 U.S. 417 (1998).

4. Marbury v. Madison, 5 U.S. (1 Cranch) 137, 1777 (1803).

5. Samuel A. Alito, Jr., "Using Presidential Signing Statement to Make Fuller Use of the President's Constitutionally Assigned Role in the Process of Enacting Law, Memorandum to the Litigation Strategy Working Group," Office of Legal Counsel, Department of Justice, Feb. 5, 1986, http://www.archives.gov/news/samuel-alito/accession-060-89-269/Acc060-89-269-box6-SG-LSWG-AlitotoLSWG-Feb1986.pdf.

6. Address by Attorney General Edwin Meese III, National Press Club, Washington, DC, Feb. 25, 1986.

7. E-mail to author from Christopher Kelley (Dec. 25, 2006) (on file with author).

8. Jess Bravin, "Judge Alito's View of the Presidency: Expansive Powers. Court Pick Endorsed Theory of Far-Reaching Authority; Tenet of Bush White House a Debate Over Terror Tactics," *Wall Street Journal*, Jan. 5, 2006, A1 (citing Christopher Kelley).

9. Ibid. (emphasis added).

10. Statement on Signing the Energy and Water Development Appropriations Act, 2002, Nov. 12, 2001, http://www.presidency.ucsb.edu/ws/index.php?pid=73462; Statement on Signing the National Defense Authorization Act for Fiscal Year 2002, Dec. 28, 2001. http://www.presidency.ucsb.edu/ws/index.php?pid=63433.

11. See note 8.

12. Philip Watts, "Bush Advisor Says President Has Legal Power to Torture Children," Jan. 8, 2006, http://www.informationclearing house.info/article11488.htm.

13. Hamdi v. Rumsfeld, 542 U.S. 507, 582 (2004) (J. Thomas, dissenting).

14. Myers v. United States, 272 U.S. 52 (1926) (J. Brandeis, dissenting).

15. Elizabeth Drew, "Power Grab," *New York Review of Books,* June 22, 2006, 10.

16. Department of Defense, Emergency Supplemental Appropriations to Address Hurricanes in the Gulf of Mexico, and Pandemic Influenza Act, 2006, PL 109–48, 119, Stat. 2680.

17. President's Statement on Signing of HR 2863, Department of Defense, Emergency Supplemental Appropriations to Address Hurricanes in the Gulf of Mexico, and Pandemic Influenza Act, 2006, Dec. 30, 2005. http://www.whitehouse.gov/news/releases/2005/12/2005 1230-8.html.

18. Hamdan v. Rumsfeld, 126 S.Ct. 2749, 2798 (U.S., 2006).

19. Michael Moss, "American Recalls Torment as a U.S. Detainee in Iraq," *New York Times,* Dec. 18, 2006, A1.

20. USA PATRIOT Improvement and Reauthorization Act of 2005, PL 109-177, Mar. 9, 2006, 120 Stat. 192.

21. Charlie Savage, "Bush Shuns Patriot Act in Addendum to Law, He Says Oversight Rules Are Not Binding," *Boston Globe,* Mar. 24, 2006, A1.

22. President George W. Bush, "Statement on Signing the USA PATRIOT Improvement and Reauthorization Act of 2005," Mar. 9, 2006. http://www.presidency.ucsb.edu/ws/index.php?pid=65326.

23. "Harman and Conyers Demand Administration Rescind

Patriot Act 'Signing Statement,'" Mar. 27, 2006. http://www.house .gov/list/press/ca36_harman/pr_060327_patriotact.html.

24. National Defense Authorization Act for Fiscal Year 2006, PL 109-163, Jan. 6, 2006, 119 Stat. 3136.

25. President George W. Bush, "Statement on Signing the National Defense Authorization Act for Fiscal Year 2006," Jan. 6, 2006. http://www.presidency.ucsb.edu/ws/?pid=65172.

26. Walter Dellinger, Assistant Attorney General, "Memorandum for the General Counsels of the Federal Government," *The Constitutional Separation of Powers Between the President and Congress*, 54–6, May 7, 1996, 1996 WL 876050.

27. Authorization for Use of Military Force Against Iraq Resolution of 2002, PL 107-243, Oct. 16, 2002, 116 Stat. 1498; President George W. Bush, "Statement on Signing the Authorization for Use of Military Force Against Iraq Resolution of 2002," Oct. 16, 2002, http://www.presidency.ucsb.edu/ws/index.php?pid=64386.

28. U.S. CONST., art. I, §8; see chapter one.

29. Inspector General Act of 1978, PL 95-452, Oct. 12, 1978, 92 Stat. 1101.

30. Marjorie Cohn, *Abu Ghraib General Lambastes Bush Administration*, Aug. 24, 2005. http://www.truthout.org/docs_2005/082405Z .shtml.

31. Emergency Supplemental Appropriations Act for Defense and for the Reconstruction of Iraq and Afghanistan, 2004, PL 108-106, Nov. 6, 2003, 117 Stat. 1209.

32. President George W. Bush, "Statement on Signing the Emergency Supplemental Appropriations Act for Defense and for the Reconstruction of Iraq and Afghanistan, 2004," Nov. 6, 2003. http:// www.presidency.ucsb.edu/ws/index.php?pid=64639.

33. Ronald W. Reagan National Defense Authorization Act for Fiscal Year 2005, PL 108-375, Oct. 28, 118 Stat. 1811.

34. President George W. Bush, "Statement on Signing the Ronald W. Reagan National Defense Authorization Act for Fiscal Year 2005," Oct. 28, 2004. http://www.presidency.ucsb.edu/ws/index.php?pid=72803.

35. "Statement on Signing S.1566 Into Law," Oct. 25, 1978, http://www.cnss.org/Carter.pdf.

36. See note 15.

37. Henry J. Hyde, United States-India Peaceful Atomic Energy Cooperation Act of 2006, PL 109-401, Dec. 18, 2006, 120 Stat. 2726; "President's Statement on HR 5682," the Henry J. Hyde United States-India Peaceful Atomic Energy Cooperation Act of 2006, Dec. 18, 2006. http://www.whitehouse.gov/news/releases/2006/12/20061218-12.html.

38. "Legality of the Threat or Use of Nuclear Weapons," Advisory Opinion of July 8, 1996, International Court of Justice, http://www.icj-cij.org/icjwww/idecisions/isummaries/iunanaummary960708.htm.

39. William M. Arkin, "Secret Plan Outlines the Unthinkable," *Los Angeles Times,* Mar. 10, 2002, 1.

40. "America as Nuclear Rogue" [Editorial], *New York Times,* Mar. 12, 2002, A26.

41. Lawyers' Committee on Nuclear Policy, "Threat or Use of Nuclear Weapons: Illegal Then, Illegal Now," New York, Aug. 2005. http://www.lcnp.org/disarmament/threatoruse.pdf.

42. Youngstown Sheet & Tube Co. v. Sawyer, 343 U.S. 579, 587 (1952).

43. Ibid., 635–7.

44. American Bar Association, Task Force on Presidential Signing Statements and the Separation of Powers Doctrine, Aug. 2006. http://www.abanet.org/op/signingstatements/aba_final_signing_statements_recommendation-report_7-24-06.pdf.

45. Michael Abramowitz, "Bush's Tactic of Refusing Laws Is Probed. Bar Association's Panel Criticizes President's Many Challenges to Legislation," *Washington Post,* July 24, 2006, A5.

46. "Statement of Bruce Fein Before the Senate Judiciary Committee Re: Presidential Signing Statements," June 27, 2006. http://judiciary.senate.gov/testimony.cfm?id=1969&wit_id=5482.

47. Charlie Savage, "Bush Challenges Hundreds of Laws," *Boston Globe,* Apr. 30, 2006, A1.

48. William Fisher, "Signing Away the Constitution?" Inter Press Service, June 29, 2006. http://ipsnews.net/news.asp?idnews=33805.

49. Al Gore, "Restoring the Rule of Law," Jan. 16, 2006 (Martin Luther King Day Speech). http://www.epic.org/privacy/terrorism/fisa/gorespeech0106.pdf.

50. Edward M. Kennedy, "On Wiretapping, Bush Isn't Listening to the Constitution," *Boston Globe,* Dec. 22, 2005, A19.

CONCLUSION

1. Marjorie Cohn, "First Officer Publicly Resists War," June 8, 2006, http://www.truthout.org/docs_2006/060806J.shtml.

2. 28 CFR 600.1, 600.3 (2007).

3. *See, for example,* Marjorie Cohn, "The Gonzales Indictment," Jan. 19, 2005, http://www.truthout.org/docs_05/011905A.shtml.

4. 18 USC §371 (2007); *See* Elizabeth de la Vega, *U.S. v. George W. Bush et al.* (New York: Seven Stories Press, 2006).

5. T.R. Reid, "Graner Gets 10 Years for Abuse at Abu Ghraib: Ex-Guard Said He Was Ordered to Mistreat Iraqis," *Washington Post,* Jan. 16, 2005, A01.

6. Associated Press, "Court-Martial Opens in an Iraqi Abuse Case," *New York Times,* May 13, 2005, A9; CBS News, "Abu Ghraib Sentence: 6 Months," http://www.cbsnews.com/stories/2005/05/17/iraq/main696043.shtml.

7. Jeannie Shawl, "Lynddie England Convicted on Abu Ghraib Charges," Sept. 26, 2005, http://jurist.law.pitt.edu/paperchase/2005/09/breaking-news-lynndie-england.php.

8. Associated Press, "England Sentenced to 3 Years for Prison Abuse," MSNBC, Sept. 28, 2005, http://www.msnbc.msn.com/id/9492624/.

9. Associated Press, "Second Abu Ghraib Abuse Trial Opens," May 12, 2005, http://www.foxnews.com/story/0,2933,156408,00.html.

10. David S. Cloud, "Prisoner Abuse: Seal Officer Hears Charges in Court-Martial in Iraqi's Death, *New York Times,* May 25, 2005, A6; David S. Cloud, "Navy Officer Found Not Guilty in Death of an Iraqi Prisoner," *New York Times,* May 28, 2005, A6.

11. Seth Hettena, "Prosecution Makes Case Against SEAL Lieutenant," *S.D. Union-Trib.,* May 26, 2005, B4.

12. Cloud, "Prisoner Abuse," A8.

13. David S. Cloud, "Seal Officer's Trial Gives Glimpse of C.I.A.'s Role in Abuse," *New York Times,* May 26, 2005, A12.

14. Tony Perry, "SEALs Instructed to Treat Prisoners Well," *Los Angeles Times,* May 26, 2005, A29.

15. Tim Golden, "Years After 2 Afghans Died, Abuse Case Falters," *New York Times,* Feb. 13, 2006, A1.

16. Human Rights Watch World Report 2006, Events of 2005, http://www.hrw.org/english/docs/2006/01/13/global12428.htm, 505–6.

17. Ibid., 506.

18. "Agreement for the Prosecution and Punishment of the Major War Criminals of the European Axis," Aug. 8, 1945, 82 UNTS. 279, article 6.

19. Jordan J. Paust, "Executive Plans and Authorizations to Violate International Law Concerning Treatment and Interrogation of Detainees," 43 *Colum. J Transnational L.* 811 (2005).

20. Scott Horton, "Through a Mirror, Darkly: Applying the Geneva Conventions to 'A New Kind of Warfare,'" *The Torture Debate in America,* (Karen Greenberg ed., New York: Cambridge University Press, 2005) 136, 145–6; Scott Horton, "When Lawyers Are War Criminals," ASIL Centennial Conference on the Nuremberg War Crimes Trial, Bowling Green, OH, Oct. 7, 2006, http://balkin.blog spot.com/2006/10/when-lawyers-are-war-criminals.html.

21. United States Army Field Manual, chapter 8, Section 501, 27-10.

22. *See* Marjorie Cohn, "The President and His Vice: Torturers' Puppetmasters," Nov. 7, 2005, http://www.truthout.org/docs_2006/110705I.shtml.

23. James R. Schlesinger et al., "Final Report of the Independent Panel to Review DOD Detention Operations" (2004), http://www.defenselink.mil/news/Aug2004/d20040824finalreport.pdf.

24. Human Rights Watch, "United States Getting Away with Torture? 2005, Impunity for the Architects of Illegal Policy," http://www.hrw.org/reports/2005/us0405/6.htm#_Toc101408096.htm.

25. Ibid.

26. See note16.

27. Eric Schmitt, "No Criminal Charges for Officer At Abu Ghraib Interrogations," *New York Times,* May 12, 2005, A11.

28. David S. Cloud, "Guantánamo Reprimand Was Sought, an Aide Says," *New York Times,* July. 12 2005, A16.

29. Associated Press, "Abu Ghraib Officer to Be Tried on Abuse Charges," Jan. 27, 2007.

30. Eric Schmitt, "4 Top Officers Cleared by Army in Prison Abuses. Findings on Abu Ghraib. U.S. Inquiry Closes With a Single High-Ranking Officer Punished," *New York Times,* Apr. 23, 2005, A1; Richard A. Serrano and Mark Mazzetti, "General Demoted Over Prison Scandal: Janis Karpinski of the Army Reserve Failed to Supervise Abu Ghraib Guards in Iraq, Officials Say. She Has Complained That She Is a Scapegoat," *Los Angeles Times,* May 6, 2005, A20.

31. Marjorie Cohn, "Abu Ghraib General Lambastes Bush Administration," Aug. 24, 2005, http://www.truthout.org/docs_2005/082405Z.shtml.

32. Title 22 USC. §7421 (2002).

33. Bruce Ackerman, "Two Recent Commentaries," Sept. 15, 2004, http://www.law.yale.edu/news/2102.htm.

34. Restatement (Third) on the Foreign Relations Law of The United States, §404 (1987); Jordan J. Paust, "Universality and the Responsibility to Enforce International Criminal Law," 11 *Houston Journal of International Law* 337, 340 (1989).

35. Hepting v. AT&T Corp., 439 F.Supp. 2d 974, 995 (N.D.Cal., 2006).

36. American Civil Liberties Union v. National Security Agency, 438 F.Supp. 2d 754, 781 (E.D. Mich., 2006).

37. Richard B. Schmitt, Greg Miller, and David G. Savage, "Wiretap Review Plan Is Still Unclear," *Los Angeles Times,* Jan. 19, 2007, 12.

38. Justice Department Oversight: Hearing Before the Senate Judiciary Commission, 110th Cong. (2007) (Statement of The Honorable Alberto Gonzales Attorney General of the United States, U.S. Department of Justice) 2007 WL 118223 (FDCH).

39. Alan Wirzbicki, "Congress Could Be Last Voice on Troop Surge," *Boston Globe,* Jan. 9, 2007, 2A.

40. See U.S. Public Law No. 93-559, § 38(F)-(2), The Foreign Assistance Act of 1974 (imposing a personnel ceiling of 4000 Americans in Vietnam within six months of enactment and 3000 Americans within one year); U.S. Public Law No. 98-43, § 4(a), The Lebanon Emergency Assistance Act of 1983 (mandating that the President

return to seek statutory authorization as a condition for expanding the size of the U.S. contingent of the Multinational Force in Lebanon); U.S. Public Law No. 91-652, The Supplemental Foreign Assistance Act of 1971, § 8 (prohibiting the use of any funds for the introduction of U.S. troops to Cambodia or provision of military advisors to Cambodian forces without the prior notification of the congressional leadership).

41. Skinner v. Railway Labor Executives' Association, 489 U.S. 602, 635 (1989) (Marshall, J., dissenting).

42. Quotations Page, Quotations Details: Martin Niemoller, http://www.quotationspage.com/quote/29611.html. "This quote is most often attributed to [Martin] Niemoller, but its exact source and wording is varied." Frank Dunham, "Where Hamdi Meets Moussaoui in the War on Terror," 53 *Drake L. Rev.* 839, 839 n. 3 (2005).

Acknowledgments

I am grateful to my editor, Peter Richardson, whose wisdom informed every page of this book, and to my friend and colleague Richard Falk for writing the foreword. Hugh Hamilton, Bernard Hibbitts, Shahram Vahdany, Jeffrey St. Clair, Don Hazen, Michael Albert, David Swanson, Michel Chossudovsky, and Marc Ash have brought my work to a wide audience, which made this book possible. My dean, Rudy Hasl, graciously supplied research support and moral support. Thomas Jefferson law students James Binnall, Nancy Ganadjian, and Dana Sniegocki provided invaluable research assistance, and my girlfriends Joan Andersson, Elinor Blake, Heidi Boghosian, Kathy Gilberd, Donna Sevilla, and Doris Brin Walker contributed to this project. Special thanks to Daniel Ellsberg for his helpful comments on the manuscript and to Ann Fagan Ginger for being my mentor. My high school teacher Roger Doney prepared me for my coming of age in the April Third Movement at Stanford in 1969. Thanks to my parents, Leonard Cohn and Florence Cohn, for their abiding love; to my grandmother, Bertha Weiner Cohn, whose revolutionary spirit runs in my veins; and to my loving fan and uncle, Rod Colbin. My sons, Victor and Nicolas Cohn-López, and my stepsons, David, John, and Dan Wallingford, motivate me to work for a better world. Jerry Wallingford, my husband and soulmate, was by my side every step of the way. This book was inspired by all who have been victimized by the Bush gang's illegal imperial adventures.

Index

About the Author

Marjorie Cohn lectures throughout the world and provides legal and political commentary on human rights and U.S. foreign policy for CBS News, Court TV, BBC, CNN, MSNBC, Fox News, NPR, Air America, and Pacifica Radio. She is president of the National Lawyers Guild and a professor at Thomas Jefferson School of Law, where she teaches criminal law and procedure, evidence, and international human rights law. A long-time criminal defense attorney, she co-authored *Cameras in the Courtroom: Television and the Pursuit of Justice*. She is a contributing editor to *Jurist*, *MWC News Magazine*, and *Guild Practitioner* and a frequent columnist for *AlterNet*, *Counterpunch*, *CommonDreams*, *AfterDowningStreet*, *Buzzflash*, *ZNet*, and *Global Research*. The 2005 recipient of San Diego County Bar Association's Service to Legal Education Award, she was named one of San Diego's top attorneys in academics for 2006. Professor Cohn was a legal observer in Iran on behalf of the International Association of Democratic Lawyers in 1978 and has participated in delegations to Cuba, China, and Yugoslavia. Her articles can be found at http://www.marjoriecohn.com.

Other Books from PoliPointPress

The Blue Pages:
A Directory of Companies Rated by Their Politics and Practices
Helps consumers match their buying decisions with their political values by listing the political contributions and business practices of over 1,000 companies.
$9.95, PAPERBACK.

JEFF COHEN, *Cable News Confidential:* *My Misadventures in Corporate Media*
Offers a fast-paced romp through the three major cable news channels—Fox CNN, and MSNBC—and delivers a serious message about their failure to cover the most urgent issues of the day.
$14.95, PAPERBACK.

JOE CONASON, *The Raw Deal:* *How the Bush Republicans Plan to Destroy Social Security and the Legacy of the New Deal*
Reveals the well-financed and determined effort to undo the Social Security Act and other New Deal programs.
$11.00, PAPERBACK.

STEVEN HILL, *10 Steps to Repair American Democracy*
Identifies the key problems with American democracy, especially election practices, and proposes ten specific reforms to reinvigorate it.
$11.00, PAPERBACK.

YVONNE LATTY, *In Conflict:* *Iraq War Veterans Speak Out on Duty, Loss, and the Fight to Stay Alive*
Features the unheard voices, extraordinary experiences, and personal photographs of a broad mix of Iraq War veterans, including Congressman Patrick Murphy, Tammy Duckworth, Kelly Daugherty, and Camilo Mejia.
$24.00, HARDCOVER.

PHILLIP LONGMAN, *Best Care Anywhere: Why VA Health Care Is Better Than Yours*
Shows how the turnaround at the long-maligned VA hospitals provides a blueprint for salvaging America's expensive but troubled health care system.
$14.95, PAPERBACK.

WILLIAM RIVERS PITT, *House of Ill Repute: Reflections on War, Lies, and America's Ravaged Reputation*
Skewers the Bush Administration for its reckless invasions, warrantless wiretaps, lethally incompetent response to Hurricane Katrina, and other scandals and blunders.
$16.00, PAPERBACK.

NOMI PRINS, *Jacked: How "Conservatives" Are Picking Your Pocket —Whether You Voted For Them or Not*
Describes how the "conservative" agenda has affected your wallet, skewed national priorities, and diminished America—but not the American spirit.
$12.00, PAPERBACK.

JOHN SPERLING et al., *The Great Divide: Retro vs. Metro America*
Explains how and why our nation is so bitterly divided into what the authors call Retro and Metro America.
$19.95, PAPERBACK.

CURTIS WHITE, *The Spirit of Disobedience: Resisting the Charms of Fake Politics, Mindless Consumption, and the Culture of Total Work*
Debunks the notion that liberalism has no need for spirituality and describes a "middle way" through our red state/blue state political impasse. Includes three powerful interviews with John DeGraaf, James Howard Kunstler, and Michael Ableman.
$24.00, HARDCOVER.

For more information, please visit www.p3books.com.